Adult Learning:
State Policies and Institutional Practices

by K. Patricia Cross and Anne-Marie McCartan

ASHE-ERIC Higher Education Research Report No. 1, 1984

Prepared by

 ® *Clearinghouse on Higher Education*
The George Washington University

Published by

Association for the Study of Higher Education

Jonathan D. Fife,
Series Editor

Cite as:
Cross, K. Patricia, and McCartan, Anne-Marie. *Adult Learning: State Policies and Institutional Practices.* ASHE-ERIC Higher Education Research Report No. 1. Washington, D.C.: Association for the Study of Higher Education, 1984.

The ERIC Clearinghouse on Higher Education invites individuals to submit proposals for writing monographs for the Higher Education Research Report series. Proposals must include:
1. A detailed manuscript proposal of not more than five pages.
2. A 75-word summary to be used by several review committees for the initial screening and rating of each proposal.
3. A vita.
4. A writing sample.

ISSN 0737-1292
ISBN 0-913317-10-1

ERIC Clearinghouse on Higher Education
The George Washington University
One Dupont Circle, Suite 630
Washington, D.C. 20036

ASHE Association for the Study of Higher Education
One Dupont Circle, Suite 630
Washington, D.C. 20036

This publication was prepared partially with funding from the National Institute of Education, U.S. Department of Education, under contract no. 400-82-0011. The opinions expressed in this report do not necessarily reflect the positions or policies of NIE or the Department.

ASHE-ERIC HIGHER EDUCATION RESEARCH
REPORT SERIES
CONSULTING EDITORS

Richard Lonsdale
Professor of Educational Administration
New York University

Linda Koch Lorimer
Associate General Counsel
Yale University

Virginia B. Nordby
Director
Affirmative Action Programs
University of Michigan

Eugene Oliver
Director, University Office of School & College Relations
University of Illinois–Champaign

Harold Orlans
Lawyer

Marianne Phelps
Assistant Provost for Affirmative Action
The George Washington University

Gary K. Probst
Professor of Reading
Prince Georges Community College

Robert A. Scott
Director of Academic Affairs
State of Indiana Commission for Higher Education

Cliff Sjogren
Director of Admissions
University of Michigan

Al Smith
Assistant Director of the Institute of Higher Education &
    Professor of Instructional Leadership & Support
University of Florida

CONTENTS

Executive Summary	**1**
Introduction	**5**
Providers	**10**
Relationships within Formal Education Structures	12
Relationships between Higher Education and Business/Industry	17
Relationships between Higher Education and Professional Associations and Labor Unions	25
Relationships between Higher Education and Community Organizations	29
Conclusion	30
Access	**32**
Participation in Adult Education	32
Barriers to Participation in Adult Education	37
Targeted Subpopulations	39
Providing Information about Adult Educational Opportunities	44
Student Costs	48
Distance Education through Communications Technologies	59
Quality Assurance	**69**
Off-Campus Degree Programs	71
State Actions	74
Programs on Military Bases	76
Nontraditional Methods	80
Conclusion	88
Revitalizing the Economy through Education	**90**
State Activities	92
Policy Questions	107
State Roles	**119**
The Laissez-Faire Approach	121
Encouragement	122
Intervention	125
Direct Support and Services	127
Summary	129
References	**138**

FOREWORD

The ERIC Clearinghouse on Higher Education and the Association for the Study of Higher Education are grateful to the Kellogg Foundation for providing the support that allowed for the publication of this special expanded issue of the ASHE-ERIC Higher Education Research Report Series. Normally these reports are kept to approximately 100 pages in order to provide a comprehensive, yet succinct review and analysis of a major issue concerning higher education. However, because of the importance of adult learning to the future of higher education, it was decided that for this one issue the length limitation would be lifted in order to fully cover the analyses conducted by K. Patricia Cross, Chair of Administration, Planning, and Social Policy at Harvard University and Anne-Marie McCartan, Project Director of the Transfer Opportunities Program at Roxbury Community College.

As reported in a recent issue of *Higher Education and National Affairs* (6/18/84), from 1972 to 1982 the participation of adults between 25 and 34 years old increased in academe by 69.8 percent, and of the population over 35 years old by 77.4 percent. Reasons for these increases have been well articulated in scholarly journals and in the general press. One new development is a heightened awareness by public officials of the relationship between higher education, adult learning, and the economy of the state or locale. This realization is causing more interest, participation, and control at the state level.

A major issue that undergirds this report is the question of leadership. Because of the importance of adult learning to the state, both the state legislative and executive branches have a responsibility for setting policies. But because the actual learning activities occur at the institutional level, institutions must not only implement the state policies but ensure that they are realistic and productive. Hence the leadership responsibility in adult learning needs to be a shared one, with institutions being both reactive as well as proactive in establishing a positive, effective climate for adult learning.

Jonathan D. Fife
Series Editor
Professor and Director
ERIC Clearinghouse on Higher Education
The George Washington University

PREFACE AND ACKNOWLEDGMENTS

This report is an outgrowth of the Lifelong Learning Project funded by the W. K. Kellogg Foundation and administered under the auspices of the Education Commission of the States (ECS). Under that project, which began in March 1980, six pilot states and 27 "associate" states considered and experimented with appropriate roles for the state in planning and delivering educational services for adults.

This report grew out of the desire to cast a net beyond the experiences of the pilot states to determine the range of problems that confronted state agencies in planning for lifelong learning and to explore the roles available to them. Additional funding from the Kellogg Foundation made it possible for us to spend several months reviewing documents from across the nation, published as well as unpublished, formal as well as informal.

Many publications are available to relate the projects and experiences of the pilot states (see Cross and Hilton 1983 for an annotated bibliography). This report uses those publications as a part of our survey of the literature, but this monograph strives for breadth rather than depth. We attempt to identify a very broad range of concerns and to illustrate the variety of state roles in addressing those concerns.

We are grateful to the Kellogg Foundation for funding, to the directors of the lifelong learning projects in the six pilot states for providing both information and inspiration, and to William J. Hilton, Director of the Kellogg Lifelong Learning Project, for his continuing help and support. In addition, we would like to express our appreciation to the many colleagues in states across the nation who sent us materials, discussed issues with us, and in other ways provided the grist for our mill.

Special thanks go to Patrick Callan, Morris Keaton, and Norman Kurland, whose knowledge and insights of the "working front" of the lifelong learning movement helped greatly in the final review of the manuscript.

Cambridge, Massachusetts
April 1984

K. Patricia Cross
Anne-Marie McCartan

EXECUTIVE SUMMARY

Adult education is the most rapidly growing segment in all
education, increasing by 17 percent between 1978 and
1981. Only about half of the growth can be attributed to
larger numbers of adults in the population; the remaining
half is attributed to the increased need and desire of adults
to continue learning. In 1981, the National Center for Education Statistics (NCES) estimates that 21 million adults
participated in some organized educational activity.

In some states, participation by adults in educational
activities is high even in the absence of comprehensive
planning and initiatives for lifelong learning per se. These
states would point to years of generous support for public
education, easy access to educational institutions like community colleges, and relatively low tuition as important
reasons why they are moving toward a Learning Society.
Other states have adopted goals and initiated efforts specifically intended to enhance learning opportunities for adults
in the state. In still another group of states, adults are not
participating in great numbers and no comprehensive planning and goal setting are taking place.

*In 1981 . . .
21 million
adults
participated in
some
organized
educational
activity.*

Yet a review of a wide assortment of state documents
indicates that, no matter what the level of participation or
extent of planning and goal setting, states are being confronted with issues related to the increased presence of
adults as learners. These issues can be grouped under four
overarching concerns: providers, access, quality assurance, and economic revitalization.

Providers

An increasing number and variety of providers are offering
opportunities for learning to adults. In 1981, 46 percent of
all courses taken by adults were provided by nonschools—
for example, business and industry, labor and professional
associations, government agencies, and community organizations. Most states, however, have only the vaguest idea
about the educational opportunities available to adults.
They could profit from more information to determine
what is distinctive about the missions of the various providers, the extent of overlap, whether competition for
adults is constructive or destructive, and which segments
of the population are being served.

States have become involved in issues concerning relationships between providers *within* the formal education

system. Most states have taken some steps to avoid duplication and "unfair" competition arising from the proliferation of off-campus centers within their boundaries. Actions range from collecting and distributing information to institutions in the hope that it will curb duplication, to curbing funding for off-campus centers. Almost all states are making conscientious efforts to promote cooperation and collaboration among schools and colleges at local levels.

States are less involved in relationships between higher education and business and industry. The line between the "training" offered by employers and the "education" offered by colleges is becoming less clear. States are just beginning to address blurred and overlapping missions among the various providers.

Access
Access to postsecondary education for young people has long been a major concern of state officials, but the gap between adults with little education and those who have more and want still more continues to grow. A college graduate is five times as likely to participate in some form of organized instruction as a high school dropout. The reasons for this phenomenon are complex, but states concerned with lowering barriers to adult education do have several options.

First, they can offer special programs for targeted subpopulations that are perceived to "need" education. States have been particularly active in offering programs for adult illiterates or functional illiterates, non-English-speaking adults, adults served by vocational rehabilitation programs, and the elderly.

Second, they can help link potential learners with available opportunities through establishing statewide information systems. Education information centers, originally authorized and funded by the federal government, are being maintained in some states despite the cessation of federal funding.

Third, they can keep costs low and support high for offerings considered to benefit the public. Approaches include low tuition at community colleges, financial aid programs for part-time students, and significant state subsidy for courses deemed important for adults.

Fourth, states can support efforts to take education to learners in isolated or underserved areas through distance delivery mechanisms. A few states are involved in full sponsorship of telecommunication delivery systems, but most are simply providing support services to institutional efforts.

Quality Assurance

Many educators and policy makers are calling for new forms of quality assessment for programs designed to serve the unique learning needs of adults. So far, almost all of the attention to quality in adult programming has gone to programs or procedures that result in degree credit, particularly off-campus programs. The question "What is quality?" appears to be straightforward and objective, when in fact it is neither. Significantly, those involved most deeply in the study of the problem are somewhat more inclined to use flexible language and recognize legitimate differences in on-campus and off-campus programs than those who are just beginning to look at the problem.

As adults increasingly use options for credit by taking examinations, by an assessment of experiential learning, and by taking courses offered by noncollegiate providers, states not already doing so will have to consider quality assurance in these nontraditional procedures.

Economic Revitalization through Education

The recent interest in revitalizing state economies through the development of human resources may prove to be one of the most substantial boosts to adult education of all state activities. Efforts are especially focused on having an available labor pool armed with skills appropriate to attracting high-technology businesses and industry. Adults have been the beneficiaries of many state-sponsored retraining programs, as today's workers are expected to constitute over 90 percent of the nation's workforce in 1990.

Support for job-training programs for displaced workers may result in lower unemployment rates and new businesses' entering a state. But some economists, manpower planners, and politicians are pointing out the need to look beyond *program* solutions to enactment of *policies* for industrial and human development. Although it is generally acknowledged that the nature and structure of the nation's economy is changing, no consensus has been reached as to just what these changes mean for educating and training America's workforce.

State Roles

No attempt is made in this monograph to determine the most typical or common state reactions and concerns about lifelong learning. How each state approaches issues highlighted in this report will depend on a number of factors. For any of these issues, a state can take one of four generalized approaches.

The laissez-faire or hands-off approach involves no state intervention, either because the state has determined that free market forces should prevail or because the issue has not yet needed resolution.

States may choose to enhance adults' learning opportunities by encouragement. The state provides no direct support, nor does it seek to intrude into the activities of educational providers. Instead, it engages in planning and goal setting, collecting data, promoting local cooperation, or establishing task forces.

In some cases, states justify intervention in issues of adult education because of the state's interest in efficient use of public resources and in protecting students against fraudulent or shoddy educational practices. States have sometimes chosen to delegate some responsibilities for coordination to the local level, but in other cases they seek to retain that authority at the state level.

Finally, in some instances states decide to become directly involved in supporting or providing adult learning services. It may be more cost-effective to offer a service statewide than locally, and it may result in the more equitable provision of services.

Even without a systematic approach to determining prevalent state roles, some general impressions result. Overall, encouragement seems to be the most common approach states use in reacting to issues of adult education. Direct support and services are often used to promote access and to initiate economic revitalization. A number of states have chosen intervention to deal with issues of educational providers and quality assurance. The range of possible state responses presented in this monograph may be helpful to state and educational leaders in thinking about appropriate state roles in adult education.

INTRODUCTION

In 1976, the U.S. Congress passed the Lifelong Learning
Act (Title I-B of the 1976 Higher Education Amendments),
which gave high visibility to the need for lifelong learning.
In passing the act, Congress was affirming that:

- *The American people need lifelong learning to enable
  them to adjust to social, technological, political, and
  economic changes.*
- *Learning takes place through formal and informal
  instruction, through educational programs conducted
  by public and private educational and other institutions and organizations, through independent study,
  and through the efforts of business, industry, and
  labor.*
- *Planning is necessary at the national, state, and local
  levels to assure effective use of existing resources in
  . . . light of changing characteristics and learning
  needs of the population.*
- *American society should have as a goal the availability of appropriate opportunities for lifelong learning
  for all its citizens without regard to restrictions of
  previous education or training, sex, age, handicapping condition, social or ethnic background, or economic circumstance* (U.S. Department of Health,
  Education, and Welfare 1978, p. C-1).

Very little money was actually appropriated, however:
Inflation, unemployment, the budget, and a change in national administrations combined to place the federal role in
lifelong learning on the back burner in the 1980s. Yet despite the lack of federal initiatives, adult education has
continued to grow.[1] Indeed, it is the most rapidly growing
segment in all education, increasing by 17 percent between
1978 and 1981 (NCES 1983). Only about half of the growth
can be attributed to larger numbers of adults in the population; the remaining half is attributable to the increased
need and desire of adults to continue learning. More than

---

[1]Adult education, as defined by the National Center for Education Statistics, refers to all courses and organized educational activities, excluding
those taken by full-time students in programs leading to a high school diploma or an academic degree. It also excludes courses taken as part of
occupational training programs lasting six months or more. Adults are defined as persons 17 years of age or older.

half (60 percent) of all courses are taken for reasons related to one's job (NCES 1983). The overwhelming numbers of participants are employed young adults between the ages of 25 and 34, and the participation rate is especially high among professionals serving the general public—43 percent of health workers, 39 percent of physicians and dentists, 37 percent of elementary and high school teachers.

The reasons for the boom in adult education are many, and forces from different directions seem to be additive.

- The demographic shift to an older population is placing the baby boom in the age of greatest adult learning activity, but it is also stimulating schools and colleges to seek new markets to replace the declining numbers of young people in the population. Schools and colleges provide 54 percent of the courses taken by adults.
- The knowledge explosion is creating new information so rapidly that job skills and knowledge are becoming obsolete in ever shorter periods of time.
- Training and education programs in business and industry are growing rapidly. In 1981, nearly one-fourth of all adult education courses were provided by the employer, and employers were sources of funding, in full or in part, for 41 percent of the courses taken by men and 26 percent of those taken by women (NCES 1983).
- Social movements for equal opportunities in work and education are increasing the need, the motivation, and the opportunities for further education. Women are the most active adult learners of any subpopulation. At all age levels, educational levels, and income levels, they exceed the proportion of male adult learners; 54 percent of the courses they take are for job-related reasons (NCES 1983). Blacks and Hispanics aged 25 to 34 are approaching the participation rate for the entire adult population, but minorities are still seriously underrepresented in adult education.
- The educational attainment of the populace is rising and with it the demand for lifelong learning. A college graduate is roughly five times as likely to be participating in adult education as a high school dropout (NCES 1983). Among persons 25 and older in 1981, 70

percent were at least high school graduates, compared with only 55 percent in 1970. This sharp increase resulted from the replacement of older, less educated cohorts by younger, more educated cohorts plus the continued rise in high school completions—up from 74 percent in 1970 to 86 percent in 1981 for persons between 25 and 34 years of age (U.S. Bureau of the Census 1982). For the most active age cohort of adult learners (25 to 34), the proportion with at least some college education grew from 30 percent to 45 percent in the single decade of the 1970s (U.S. Bureau of the Census 1982).

- Adult education is growing more rapidly among the elderly (which is also a rapidly growing proportion of the population) than among any other age group—a 29 percent increase in the three years from 1978 to 1981 (NCES 1983).

For all of these reasons, participation in adult education is growing without any sustained attention to it from the once-promising Lifelong Learning Act. If adults are seeking education as never before, business and industry are supporting it as never before, and schools and colleges are pursuing it as never before, why should state policy makers concern themselves? One school of thought is that as long as the free market seems to be doing so well, perhaps states and the federal government should stay out of it. Many state policy makers, however, are finding it almost impossible to remain detached from this phenomenon, which promises to have a dramatic impact on equal opportunity, the quality and coordination of education, and the economic future of the state.

The forces that seem to be pulling states into some concern about planning for lifelong learning are in many cases the flip side of the reasons for the growth of adult education.

- If adult education becomes increasingly important to jobs and upward career mobility, what will happen to adults who do not participate (which seem to be the poor, the unemployed, the poorly educated, and minorities)? What is the state's obligation to ensure access to equal educational and job opportunities?

- If the death of younger people in the population is causing schools and colleges and private entrepreneurs to compete vigorously for the growing adult education market, what obligation does the state have to maintain quality and ensure consumer protection against exaggerated claims and poor educational quality?
- If the economic vitality of the state in the new technological age depends on the development of human resources, how will the state ensure that it is in a competitive position to attract industry to the state and that the state is developing the necessary human capital for the future?
- If adult learning is decentralized, uncoordinated, and diffused throughout a variety of agencies, can the state assist in avoiding wasteful overlap and destructive competition, and can communication and coordination make a more efficient system for providers and learners?

States are beginning to address these issues, although there is no consensus among the states on which issues related to lifelong learning are most important. (Perhaps the explanation is that none of the literature tends to coalesce opinions.) Few states have grappled with any comprehensive planning on lifelong learning, and issues tend to emerge ad hoc and appear fairly idiosyncratic state by state.

No state has developed a comprehensive policy on the provision of learning opportunity for adults that includes new institutional structures, new patterns of institutional support, new student-aid policies, new academic services, new academic policies—in admissions and transfer, for example—and new and more comprehensive forms of coordination with respect to lifelong learning. No state has developed an integrated set of policies that regards the provision of learning opportunities for adults as an imperative state need and encourages adult learning as the cornerstone of such a policy (Jonsen 1978, p. 362).

Even today, only one state, New York, has developed a comprehensive set of goals for lifelong education in the year 2000 (see Appendix A), although most states have by now grappled with policies in several of the areas Jonsen mentioned.

The issue of lifelong learning encompasses five broad areas related to providers, access, quality assurance, the economy, and state roles, each of which is addressed in one of the remaining chapters in this monograph. The next four chapters open with examples of the types of questions confronting state officials. The final chapter is an attempt to synthesize states' responses to the issues raised by the increased presence of adults as learners.

- How do states resolve the battles for turf between providers of adult basic education?
- Should a state use a common rate of reimbursement for all providers?
- To what lengths should states go to promote closer ties between education and business and industry?

One of the reasons adult education has been growing without any concerted effort on the part of policy makers in state and federal government is that much of adult education occurs outside the formal educational establishment of schools and colleges. In 1981, 46 percent of all courses taken by adults were provided by institutions other than schools—for example, business and industry, labor and professional associations, government agencies, community organizations. No one knows for sure how fast the extraeducational sector is growing or how extensive it has become, but it is estimated that private and public employers spend roughly $30 billion a year on educational and training programs, and the federal government alone reported 33.3 million hours of training for its over 2 million civilian employees in 1979 (Craig and Evers 1981).

The education work done outside the formal school system has been called "the shadow educational system" because so little is known about it (Lusterman 1977). But it is now emerging from the shadows. The National Center for Education Statistics has recently announced plans to add two new categories to its collection of information about education. One will include employer-related organizations like corporations and government agencies; the other will include service-oriented organizations like libraries, museums, and professional associations (*Chronicle of Higher Education* 25 May 1983).

A growing number of states are also beginning to recognize the educational role of "other providers." To date that recognition largely takes the form of collecting information about what is being offered by whom and offering "official encouragement" for providers at local levels to work together. Only one state—New York—has a structure that accommodates most of the public providers of educational services under one body, which includes 721 public libraries, 750 museums and historical societies, nine educational television stations, and 44 Boards of Cooperative Educational Services, as well as the continuing education programs of schools and colleges (Kurland 1983).

Most planners, however, face a vast array of providers, uncounted and uncoordinated by any central agency. Types of learning include core skills (for example, basic literacy or high school diploma), vocational skills, two-year or four-year undergraduate degrees, graduate or professional postgraduate degrees, and continuing education. That learning can be provided by an array of organizations ranging from traditional colleges and universities through vocational schools, labor unions, the armed services, prisons, museums, and religious organizations, to name just a few (Kurland, Purga, and Hilton 1982, p. 13).

Table 1 gives vivid testimony to the diversity of adult education. No single agency provides more than a fifth of the courses taken by adults, and the formal school system provides just a little over half of all adult education courses (NCES 1982)—that vast system of noncredit courses and workshops ranging from adult basic education to Chinese cooking to advanced seminars for tax attorneys. Further, employers play a substantial role in the education and training of adults, providing almost one-fourth of all adult education courses and contributing some funding for a third of the courses (NCES 1982).

Most state officials have only the vaguest idea about the educational opportunities available to adults. At a minimum, it seems that more information is desirable to determine what is distinctive about the missions of the various providers, the extent of overlap, whether competition for adult learners is constructive or destructive, and which segments of the population are being served. These issues lead to innumerable questions concerning the states' appropriate role in coordinating, regulating, mediating, and funding the various lifelong learning options.

Because postsecondary education is a state responsibility, perhaps the best way to tackle the new questions created for statewide planning by the multiple providers of adult education is to look at the relationships between higher education and the other major providers of adult education. These relationships can be discussed under four headings: (1) relationships among institutions *within* the formal educational system; (2) relationships between

Private and public employers spend roughly $30 billion a year on educational and training programs.

TABLE 1

PROVIDERS OF INSTRUCTION AND MAJOR SOURCES OF FUNDING FOR ADULT EDUCATION COURSES, YEAR ENDING MAY 1981

Item	Number of Courses Taken (000)	Percentage Distribution
Total courses taken, by provider of instruction	*37,381*	*100.0*
School	**20,154**	**53.9**
Elementary/secondary school	2,551	6.8
Vocational/trade school	3,413	9.1
2-year institution	7,030	18.8
4-year institution	7,160	19.2
Nonschool	**17,227**	**46.1**
Business/industry	5,119	13.7
Labor/professional association	1,858	5.0
Government agency	2,934	7.8
Community organization	3,172	8.5
Tutor	1,637	4.4
Other	2,507	6.7
Employer was provider	*9,260*	*24.8*
Total courses taken, by source of funding	*37,381*	*100.0*
Self or family	17,760	47.5
Government or public funding	6,402	17.1
Business/industry	8,090	21.6
Other source	5,129	13.8
Employer was one source	*12,287*	*32.9*

Source: National Center for Education Statistics 1982.

higher education and business/industry; (3) relationships between higher education and labor unions and professional associations; and (4) relationships between higher education and community organizations.

Relationships within Formal Education Structures
Relationships within the formal educational system appear to be moving from independence through competition to cooperation. Competition between educational institutions

has been created by the lack of traditional college students but also by the blurring of educational missions. When education was age-graded, young people moved vertically from elementary school to high school to college, and each level had its own distinctive market, making independence the predominant relationship. Today, however, every level of education serves, in one way or another, adult students. Most school districts have adult schools, most community colleges have a majority of part-time adult students plus extensive community education programs, and most four-year colleges have been expanding their extension and continuing education divisions. Some markets are distinctive; others are very similar. The extension division of the University of California, for example, serves primarily adults who already have a first degree. At the University of California at Berkeley, 78 percent of those enrolled in extension courses have a first college degree, and half of those have graduate or professional degrees (Stern 1983). Thus, the market of the University of California extension division is distinct from other educational institutions; competition for the division comes largely from the continuing education programs of professional associations.

Although few states have conducted the necessary studies, it is possible to determine the markets, distinctive and overlapping, among institutions of postsecondary education. When the Ohio Board of Regents (1982d) conducted a study of noncredit continuing education offerings in 115 Ohio postsecondary institutions, they found that most colleges were offering primarily courses and workshops emphasizing skills and professional development; that is, 48 percent of all noncredit offerings serving 51 percent of all registrants were basically job-related. Although the numbers were too small to be much more than suggestive, the more distinctive markets seem to have been carved out by the emphasis in Ohio's private two-year colleges on personal and intellectual development (65 percent of their offerings) and in four-year private colleges on cultural, recreational, and avocational areas (42 percent of their offerings). More than half of the offerings of technical colleges, university branches, and four-year public colleges were in skills and professional development, albeit presumably at different levels of accomplishment. Community colleges seem to be serving their comprehensive function by showing the most even distribution across the five categories—skill and professional development, 31 percent; personal/intellectual development, 17 percent; personal and family living, 17 percent; society and community awareness, 7 percent; and cultural/recreational/avocational development, 28 percent. This information, now collected annually in Ohio, suggests that postsecondary institutions may be seeking distinctive markets, serving different kinds of needs and populations at different levels of career and professional development.

One of the most emotional issues to strike higher education in recent years is the proliferation of off-campus centers. Two aspects of this issue have been the source of acrimony within the formal educational system. One is the issue of assuring quality (discussed later in this monograph). The other is the issue of competition and duplication. In a recent inventory, the California Postsecondary Education Commission found 4,500 locations within its state boundaries where college courses, including certificate and external degree programs, were offered by both public and independent institutions (Education Commission of the States 1981).

Some colleges literally have awakened one morning to find an "off-campus center" from an institution possibly hundreds of miles away in their backyard. The problem is especially severe where tuition differs greatly, and it tends to be especially complex when institutions cross state lines. The various steps taken by accrediting associations and state agencies to assure quality do not really address the issue of competition and duplication unless one assumes that "good" programs tend to drive out "bad" ones. But three "good" off-campus programs competing for the same market may not be the best use of scarce educational resources.

The need for greater communication and cooperation extends across state boundaries. A recent FIPSE (Fund for the Improvement of Postsecondary Education) project established two new regional consortiums to try to improve access, reduce competition and duplication, and make more efficient use of personal and material resources (Martorana and Kuhns 1983). The increased efforts going into coordination at almost every level are not concerned only with adult education, but the phenomenon of taking education to location-bound working adults has certainly exacerbated the problems of duplication and competition in recent years.

By this time, most states have taken some steps to avoid duplication and "unfair" and destructive competition arising from the proliferation of off-campus centers within their boundaries. Actions range from collecting and distributing information to institutions in the hope that it will control duplication (Education Commission of the States 1981, p. 498) to curbing funding for off-campus courses. The Texas legislature, for example, attached a rider to the state appropriations bill reducing funding for off-campus centers by 25 to 35 percent. The 35 percent reduction takes effect as the number of off-campus courses increases beyond 7 percent of the institution's total semester hours (Education Commission of the States 1981, p. 525). Texas also enacted statutory provisions to restrict the expansion of branch campus operations by private institutions of higher education. Such broadside controls, inserted into legislation, would appear to have the potential for removing possibly important access to educational opportunity and for discouraging "good," nonduplicative programs as well as less desirable programs.

Between the laissez-faire approach and the curtailment of funding lie a number of other ways to deal with the proliferation of off-campus programs. Most common are program review procedures, aimed at both quantity and quality and the creation of "coordinating districts." Using a staff review procedure, Alabama brought about a reduction in the production of off-campus credit hours by 61 percent between 1978 and 1980, maintaining that quality had increased substantially; that reduction in off-campus credit hours continued in 1981 (Education Commission of the States 1981, p. 446; 1982, p. 30).

No evidence suggests that off-campus courses are, as a group, inferior to on-campus courses. In some areas, however, unnecessary duplication, waste, and poor quality have been apparent. A well-designed review that considers both access and quality would seem to be an appropriate state role for achieving quality while reducing unnecessary duplication among institutions.

Potential "turf wars" can also be reduced by making one provider a local coordinator. Kentucky makes a state university responsible for an extended-campus coordinating district. The university's task is to assess the need, ensure adequate offerings, use existing resources, and provide liaison with other institutions and with the Council on Higher Education. Community colleges within the University of Kentucky community college system are restricted to offering extended campus instruction in their home counties, and four-year public universities may not offer lower-division instruction within 30 miles of a community college.

Another approach that seems to have promise is to control the number and type of new degree programs when they are first proposed. The Illinois Board of Higher Education requires colleges and universities intending to offer a degree program at a new site to notify the board so that it can notify other colleges of the proposal. If a request is received within 60 days following the notice of intent, the proposing institution must host a conference for all interested parties to discuss and coordinate the proposal (Illinois Board of Higher Education 1983).

Understandably, most states prefer to settle turf wars locally. In fact, the Vermont Higher Education Planning Commission, after extensive study, took the explicit position that planning for all adult education should be done regionally and locally rather than statewide. The commission recommended the creation of regional councils for postsecondary adult education where such councils do not already exist and created a task force to promote regional cooperation (Education Commission of the States 1981, p. 527).

Local planning groups tend to be defined by function (for example, adult basic education or postsecondary education) or by geographical boundaries (community college districts, for example)—sometimes both. Illinois, for example, has established local planning districts for adult elementary and high school completion programs that are congruent with existing community college boundaries, thereby defining the planning group by both function and geography. California assigns the function of adult high school completion programs to school districts but permits the flexibility for community colleges to handle this function if such a plan is mutually agreed upon locally.

Most states have already assumed coordinating and regulating functions for public educational institutions. Adult education represents an expansion of these roles, as it greatly increases the possible areas for competition and overlap. No problems of "coordination" between school districts and community colleges existed until adults became a common target. Similarly, off-campus degree programs are a phenomenon brought about by the educational activities of working adults. The missions and markets of schools and colleges that were once clear are less so now. But at least in the formal educational system, it is a matter of getting educators to cooperate with fellow educators. Gaining cooperation, coordination, or even communication among providers from different sectors of society, however, is a different matter.

Relationships between Higher Education and Business/Industry

Ten years ago, no one would have foreseen any competition between the "training" offered by employers and the "education" offered by colleges. But with the new emphasis on the development of human relations in industry and colleges' new interest in adult learners, traditional missions are becoming blurred. "As we become a learning society, it becomes progressively more difficult to decide where the university ends and the corporate world begins and where they both fit within the larger education and training system . . ." (Gold 1981, p. 9).

Within the past decade, industry has become involved in granting academic degrees, offering courses redeemable for college credit, building campuses with dormitories and well-equipped classrooms, "developing the whole person" through education, and creating large education and training departments with hundreds of people working full-time on instructional programs for adults. Industry has been engaging in many educational activities that used to be the sole province of formal education.

- The Boston area alone has at least four degree-granting institutions founded by such noncolleges as a hospital, a manufacturer of computers, a consulting firm, and a banking institute. These institutions are not in-house degree programs for employees; they have been authorized by the state to grant associate, baccalaureate, or masters degrees to anyone meeting their requirements for admission.

- Academic institutions are increasingly likely to accept for credit courses offered by corporations. A recent catalog of the American Council on Education's Office on Educational Credit and Credentials lists over 2,000 courses offered by more than 180 corporations that appear, to faculty examiners from academe, worthy of college credit.
- Xerox, IBM, AT&T, McDonald's, and a host of other corporate giants have built campuses with well-equipped classrooms and spacious residence halls complete with dining halls and recreation facilities. In 1979, for example, more than 20,000 people attended classes taught by 130 full-time instructors at the Leesburg, Virginia, campus of Xerox (Dinkelspiel 1981).
- Many descriptions of courses and institutes sound more like "education" than like "training." For example, the educational philosophy of the IBM Systems Research Institute "is in many ways that of a university. It stresses fundamental and conceptual education and allows students to choose those courses that will best nurture their own development" (IBM Systems Research Institute 1981, p. 6).
- Industry has been developing a new profession of "corporate trainers." Xerox has 1,400 full-time training personnel located at 12 training centers around the world (Dinkelspiel 1981, p. 93). Their instructional techniques are at least as sophisticated as those of many college teachers and their instructional materials and equipment frequently much better. The American Society for Training and Development (ASTD) has become an influential professional association. Its membership has doubled over the past decade to 21,000 national members, with about 20,000 additional people who are members of ASTD's local chapters (Craig and Evers 1981).
- In 1982, AT&T alone spent over $6 million on remedial programs for 14,000 employees. Much of the education provided was in basic academic skills at the ninth grade level.

At the same time that industry is providing some of the educational services once provided by formal educational institutions, colleges and universities have been expanding their educational services into areas once occupied by employers and other providers.

- In 1967–68, 1,102 colleges offered noncredit programs for adults. By 1975–76, the number increased to 2,225 colleges and by 1979–80 to 2,285 colleges or 72 percent of the institutions of higher education in the United States (NCES 1983). An Ohio survey of noncredit courses offered by colleges in that state showed the objective of the majority of courses was to develop job skills or enhance professional development (Ohio Board of Regents 1982a).
- The overwhelming majority of today's college students are attending college for job-related reasons, and the predominant shift in curriculum has been from liberal arts and general education to vocational and professional training. In community colleges, the ratio of associate degrees conferred in occupational curricula shifted from 40 percent in 1970 to 60 percent by 1980 (Cohen and Brawer 1982, p. 203).
- Many courses offered by colleges are "training" courses that might once have been considered on-the-job training. For example, one community college offers a course in airline reservations, which "prepares students for airline employment opportunities through a familiarization of the procedures involved in airline reservations, the use of official airline guides, and airline route structures."

The point of these examples is that the missions of various educational providers, once reasonably distinct, are increasingly blurred, increasing the potential for competition and cooperation among providers and decreasing the likelihood of the third option, independence.

The rapid increase in the numbers of part-time learners is another factor that is increasing the potential for competition and/or cooperation among providers of educational services. The programs of industry, once confined to full-time working adults, and the programs of colleges, once confined largely to dependent postadolescents, are now serving roughly the same market. Formerly full-time workers are becoming part-time students, and formerly full-time students are becoming part-time workers. The result is that increasing numbers of people—young, middle-aged, and elderly—are combining work and study during the lifespan (Cross 1981, Ch. 1).

Further adding to the blurring of educational function is the rise of a new profession, the vendor of educational services. Vendors are independent profit-making firms or individuals who contract with employers and sometimes with educational institutions to provide workshops, courses, training programs, and consulting. About one-fourth of the industries surveyed in one study used outside vendors in employee training programs. For training programs for exempt employees, 48 percent of the firms reported they used an outside private training specialist, 9 percent used vocational, technical, or business school teachers, and 27 percent used college and university professors (Craig and Evers 1981, p. 40).

The use of college teachers as private entrepreneurial vendors is an underground activity that has profound implications for educational institutions. Growing numbers of teachers and professors have established local and national reputations as training specialists and consultants on training. Corporations frequently find it far easier, more satisfactory, and less costly to make arrangements directly with the college faculty member of their choice than to go through the complicated procedures and inevitable delays of academic decision making and the expense of college overhead. Colleges, unless they can deal more promptly and realistically with corporate training officers, stand to lose money, faculty time, and faculty commitment.

States are just beginning to address blurred and overlapping missions among the various providers, and the problems are addressed in a great variety of ways, all pointing toward three possible options: (1) to encourage greater differentiation of function or mission through taking some stand on which providers should perform which functions; (2) to encourage or permit free-market competition among providers; or (3) to encourage collaboration and joint planning among providers.

Option one: Encouraging greater differentiation

South Carolina (although not a precise illustration of option one) has attracted industry to the state by providing state financing for community and technical colleges to "design and operate education/training programs to prepare to industry's quality specifications and lead time, the workforce necessary to enable the new incoming industries and existing expanding industries to start up in the black and profit at the onset" (Garrison 1980, p. 21). The 16 technical colleges in South Carolina have adopted a three-point program in responding to the needs of employers: (1) special schools training for a new or expanding industry, (2) ongoing occupational programs to prepare skilled craftsmen and technicians to meet industry's and business's future needs, and (3) continued upgrading and retraining programs to keep pace with changing technology (Garrison 1980, p. 21). With the state's assuming responsibility for an adequately trained workforce, industry has less incentive to provide education/training programs, which tends to keep clear the distinctions between "educators" and "employers."

Increasing numbers of people—young, middle-aged, and elderly—are combining work and study during the lifespan.

Another way to define nonoverlapping missions for schools and employers is to promise that the educational sector will provide all education in basic skills for the workforce, thus relieving employers of any responsibility in this area. Although the public generally assumes that the teaching of basic skills is the proper function of publicly supported education, industry is apparently finding it necessary to provide, at its expense, considerable training in the basic skills. California, for example, specifically supports the premise that noncredit programs in adult basic education, high school diploma programs, English as a Second Language, and other programs deemed to serve the "public good" should be supported with public funds.

A state could presumably sharply restrict the definition of collegiate education to nonvocational programs, assuming responsibility only for providing the general and lifelong learning skills to enable workers to learn new things as needed at the employer's or the worker's expense. That approach would sharply curtail the expanding mission of higher education and make employees' education the clear responsibility of the employer, but even granted the unlikely assumption that "nonvocational" could be adequately defined, it is probably quite an unrealistic expectation on the eve of the Information Society. No evidence suggests that states will deliberately adopt policies forcing industry into a greater share of adult education. Indeed, the trend seems quite the opposite. Schools and colleges today are spending considerable effort to slow down the education and training programs launched by business and industry by getting employers to contract with educational institutions for the services.

Option two: Encouraging free-market competition
Encouraging free-market competition among providers can range all the way from a laissez-faire nonposition (the present stance of most states) to the active encouragement of competition. Most states assume that they have no particular role in employer education programs, but many states would like to encourage industry to share the costs of adult education. It appears, for example, that most states are adopting a hands-off policy with respect to the rapidly growing practice of college representatives' encouraging employers to purchase educational and training programs from the college. If the college is permitted to keep the funds, it has an incentive to be competitive—with other colleges, private vendors, and industry itself. This is an example of unregulated, free-market economy in worker education. The employer is the judge of quality and cost-effectiveness. The job of the seller (colleges) is to be responsive to the market.

The practice of licensing noncolleges to offer full-scale degree programs appears inherently to be a policy that puts colleges and industry in direct competition. Until quite recently, higher education has had a monopoly on degrees and credit. Now, noncolleges are entering that market with the explicit permission of the state.

In Massachusetts, for example, noncolleges wishing to offer a degree may apply for authorization from the Board of Regents. The procedure is similar to that used for granting academic credit for courses offered by corporations. The application includes all supporting documents, including evidence of incorporation as a nonprofit educational institution in Massachusetts. A visiting committee conducts a one- or two-day site visit, looking at fiscal stability, curriculum, faculty, degree requirements, etc. The committee's report and recommendations are submitted to the Board of Regents, a public hearing is held, the staff makes recommendations, and ultimately the full board acts on the request. Organizations that have gone through the process and been given the authority to grant degrees include the Arthur D. Little Management Education Institute, Massachusetts General Hospital Institute of Health Professions, and Wang Institute. Presumably any organization that can establish itself as a nonprofit educational institution and meet the requirements of the Board of Regents may enter into the competition. The new wrinkle in recent applications is that corporations with a particular interest in the human capital generated in the new degree programs rather than wealthy donors and educators are forming the nonprofit institutions.

The presumed motivation for the entry of noncolleges into the degree-granting business, however, is that higher education is not training people in the areas of interest to the sponsor. As long as this premise holds true, the new institute is not a "competitor" to local institutions of higher education but has found a distinctive niche that is not being filled.

Option three: Encouraging collaboration
The most common practice in the states with respect to defining the relationship between colleges and corporations seems to be the active encouragement of collaboration and cooperation. The Ohio Board of Regents, for example, took the position that its appropriate role in planning for lifelong learning is to serve as *catalyst* in linking together the resources of higher education and the needs of learners, employers, and government. To implement this position, the board first undertook three studies: (1) a survey of noncredit continuing education offered by public and private colleges in Ohio (Ohio Board of Regents 1982a); (2) a survey of the nature and scope of training provided by business and industrial firms (Ohio Board of Regents 1982d); and (3) a survey of exemplary services provided to business by state-assisted colleges and universities at little or no cost (Ohio Board of Regents 1982c). The conclusions included the following:

- Cooperation is increasing between Ohio colleges, companies, and government agencies, but efforts can be made to expand and sharpen these links.
- Large companies in Ohio are providing most of their own training, but the rest are seeking assistance from outside vendors.
- Needed continuing education for the adult workforce can most effectively be provided through a joint effort between companies and colleges.
- A number of internal barriers within colleges and companies inhibit cooperative work-education relationships.
- More effective publicity is needed about the availability of college and university resources.
- The format of adult learning opportunities must be more flexible.
- All parties in the process need to be represented in designing and strengthening work-education relationships.
- Work-education relationships are best developed and strengthened locally or regionally.
- Education providers must collaborate to guard against duplication of effort and gaps in service and to make maximum use of all educational resources (Skinner and Moore 1983, p. 68).

In addition to funding and conducting the exploratory studies, the Ohio Board of Regents implemented its role as catalyst by sponsoring five regional conferences to bring together representatives of higher education with those from business. The board also sought to increase communication by establishing a newsletter to disseminate information about links between higher education and business and by establishing and maintaining continuing conversations between administrative staff from the Board of Regents and various providers of adult education from business and government. Finally, the board set up regional Work and Learning Councils to provide a structure for the continuing exchange of information regarding job training and opportunities among the providers and users of adult educational services in each region.

The Board of Regents clearly articulated the role of the state in planning for lifelong learning in Ohio. The board's role, as they see it, is to encourage providers and users to get together locally and regionally. It has, however, played a very active role as catalyst—conducting studies to provide basic information, bringing people together, setting up formal and informal structures for continuing conversations.

The relationship between higher education and business/ industry is changing. It is certainly no longer independent, as each segment moves steadily into realms and responsibilities once occupied by the other. Actions being taken by states are explicitly or implicitly affecting relationships between higher education and business, and now is the time to think through the options and their implications for the future.

Relationships between Higher Education and Professional Associations and Labor Unions
The relationship between established educational institutions and professional associations and labor unions is similar to that with business and industry. Competition and cooperation are increasing as the option for independence gradually fades.

Professional associations are part of the "shadow" educational system that is growing faster than most state planners realize. The competition from professional associations is felt most directly by major universities with professional schools and extension divisions that traditionally serve doctors, lawyers, engineers, and other professionals. In fact, professional associations are already reaching more adults through their educational programs than all universities combined—5 to 6 million people annually compared to 3 to 4 million people in university extension programs (Stern 1983).

Professional associations are sufficiently aggressive in their expansion of educational services that the time may come when professional associations will provide not only the increasingly necessary workshops, institutes, and courses to help working professionals keep up with new developments in their fields but will move into education for the *first* professional degree as well. "By the turn of the century, within a generation, several important universities will lose their law schools, medical schools, and other professional schools" (Stern 1979, p. 8). With the increasing emphasis on relicensure in the professions, the continuing education of professionals is becoming compulsory. Professional associations have rushed into that market and are arranging for codification of their programs with state licensing boards. The most certain way to relicensure, it must seem to many in the licensed professions, is to take the courses certified to meet the requirements of the profession.

> *The university system has been largely outflanked by what has already happened. . . . The University as an institution has no independent policy and no independent set of practical guidelines in continuing professional education. It has consented to be led by professional societies, by faculty members representing the professions who are, in turn, members of interlocking directorates—of licensing boards, and of the high command of professional societies and professional faculties simultaneously* (Stern 1979, p. 7).

Stern, as a university extension dean, has a right to be concerned, but he is not altogether parochial in his concern. Professional education is big business and growing. The American Management Association, for example, is one of the largest providers of professional education in the world. It enrolls 100,000 adults in some 3,200 workshops and seminars each year. The American Management Association, large as its educational arm is, however, controls only a small piece of the market for business education. Some 3,000 different providers put on approximately 40,000 business seminars each year.

The extensive and growing educational activities of professional associations demonstrate the enormous need for lifelong education in the professions. It may also suggest that there is more than enough demand to keep a great variety of suppliers in the business of providing everything from self-instructional materials to full-scale professional degree programs. But "universities must reach working agreements about continuing education programs with professional groups" (Stern 1983, p. 7).

Those "working agreements" are going to bring into sharp focus some critical issues. What is the appropriate balance between university faculty and practicing professionals in the instructional programs? Is equal opportunity threatened in some of the arrangements between licensing boards and their certification of the programs and materials in continuing professional education? What is the responsibility of the state to ensure the quality of professional services? Is the practice of "mandating" continuing education for licensed professionals the most effective way to ensure consumer protection? The providers of continuing education in the professions are using the media and technology extensively. What can other providers learn from these experiences? Does a solid program of research and evaluation exist?

Apparently, no state has any very effective method for ascertaining the extent and contribution of the providers of continuing professional education, and no state has any plans for considering the rational development of professional education as a vital element in lifelong learning. The contribution of professional associations is potentially very great, but states will not be able to capitalize on new opportunities for realignments or reassertions of traditional roles if the questions are not raised for discussion.

Labor unions are becoming increasingly active in bargaining for educational benefits for union members, in overseeing the access to apprenticeship training programs, and in providing direct educational services. The George Meany Center for Labor Studies, located on a 47-acre campus in Maryland, is celebrating, according to its 1983 catalog, its fifteenth year of "academic" life. So far, 30,000 students have attended classes at the residential center, which has the latest in electronic teaching aids, an evening lecture and concert series, exhibits of paintings, sculpture, and photography, a full recreation program, and a promise that "the programs, teaching methods, menus, and facilities are intended to suit a student body with an average age of 39" (George Meany Center 1983–84, p. 4). It sounds like a union model of the typical residential college campus.

The creation of a campus for the specialized curriculum of labor studies notwithstanding, labor unions in general have shown more interest in cooperating with established institutions of higher education than in developing their own programs. An especially interesting example of cooperation is the three-way cooperative model worked out among the United Auto Workers, Ford Motor Company, and approximately 65 community colleges. Last year, the Employee Development and Training Program (EDTP) was founded at Henry Ford Community College in Michigan. The new EDTP center will develop programs and educational materials to be used by local coalitions of management, unions, and community colleges in the 65 communities where UAW-Ford plants are located. The major mission of the EDTP network is to deal with unemployment and retraining of union workers. An estimated 100,000 workers will participate in the program over the years (Parnell 1982–83).

No state has apparently taken much notice of the labor unions as direct or indirect providers of educational services for adults. Yet with the arrival of the information economy and its promised use of robots, unions will be confronted with serious problems of layoffs and unemployment, and the need for retraining is increasing.

At the moment, at least, funding is not a major problem in working with labor unions. The educational funds generated by unions through contract negotiations add up to impressive amounts. Education treasure chests *within* companies run from $1.5 to $5 million per year, usually generated by the employer's contributions of 1 percent or less of the union payroll (Weinstein 1982). The other great source of untapped funds exists in tuition aid benefits. The amount of job-based tuition available in any given year for union and nonunion employees combined is as high as $6 billion. But since fewer than 5 percent of employees take advantage of the programs, only about $300,000 is used annually. The reason the money is not used, says Ivan Charner, research director for the National Institute for Work and Learning, is that employees lack information and counseling about educational benefits *(Higher Education Daily* 2 May 1983). If states were to tap those funds to serve the educational needs of workers and employers, some program of dissemination would need to be worked out among colleges, labor unions, and employers.

Labor unions seem to have defined for themselves a rather specific role as providers; their programs emphasize the preparation of union members for leadership roles in the labor movement. As education becomes increasingly important in the information economy, however, educational benefits are likely to increase, despite the fact that they are underused now. Although individual colleges have occasionally developed innovative programs in cooperation with labor unions, few state officials have encouraged the use of union benefits to provide access for blue-collar workers or even to add to the work skills of thousands of state employees who may be members of labor unions.

Relationships between Higher Education and Community Organizations

Local and community groups—city recreation departments, community organizations, churches and synagogues—provide educational services for more than 15 million people (Peterson and Associates 1979). Although individual institutions have from time to time worked on improving "town/gown" relationships through membership in and speeches to the Rotary, the Chamber of Commerce, United Way, and other local groups, until quite recently few colleges viewed community agencies as potential competitors or collaborators in the provision of educational services.

With many states now making it explicit that planning for adult education should be done locally, a question is raised as to how that should be done and who should provide the leadership for it. Local planning, of course, involves more than community agencies: It also includes school districts, employers, and other providers of learning options for location-bound adults. So far much of the planning and coordination have involved linking two providers together, for example, community colleges and secondary school districts or community colleges and local employers. Increasingly, however, states are encouraging broader-based community efforts that would bring all providers into the planning effort at once rather than creating the links pair by pair.

One problem is whether to try to establish new "neutral" agencies to coordinate the efforts of local providers or whether to assign leadership to some existing agency like the local community college, school district, or library. Some states have created new local or regional planning boards, such as the Work and Learning Councils in Ohio or the Regional Councils for Adult Postsecondary Education in Vermont (Education Commission of the States 1982,

p. 159). Others are designating local community college districts as the coordinators and planners of local efforts.

The designation of community colleges as local conveners of educational providers seems to be growing, with the active support and encouragement of the American Association of Community and Junior Colleges. Because its mission is to "identify and analyze community problems and propose solutions" (Gleazer 1980, p. 11), "the community college is uniquely qualified to become the nexus of a community learning system sufficient to respond to the population's learning needs" (p. 10). "What is required is daily communication with the business community, the county and city planning bodies, employment agencies, research organizations, the chamber of commerce, state and federal agencies, school officials, census bureaus, and the media" (p. 12).

A good example of community college districts as nexus occurs in Arizona. The Arizona Vocational Act of 1982 requires the providers of vocational education to coordinate their planning and directs Maricopa and Pima Community College Districts to provide the coordination and leadership for the cooperative planning. The community college districts have convened representatives from school districts, community colleges, private businesses, and technical schools and sponsors of employment and training programs with people from the community who could provide information about needed labor and about the skills and knowledge required for employment. Other groups represented include the Department of Corrections, the Bureau of Indian Affairs, universities, and various governmental offices. Overall, 50 to 60 people are directly involved in the planning for vocational education coordinated by the community colleges.

While it is not yet clear that community colleges are serving nationwide as the nexus for coordinating local providers, it does appear that community colleges are establishing links between themselves and other providers at a rapid rate (see Young 1981, p. 49).

Conclusion
The inescapable conclusion regarding the role of multiple providers in the Learning Society is that over the years all providers seem to have expanded their missions and activi-

ties. It is no longer clear where the educational responsibilities of schools and colleges end, nor is it clear who is providing what services for which markets. Is pre-college-level education for adults the responsibility of school districts or community colleges? With most education aimed toward improved job skills and the revitalization of the economy through development of "human capital," what are the appropriate roles of the multiple providers of vocational/technical education? Should noncolleges be offering degrees? How and where should continuing education in the professions be conducted to serve the public good? What are the appropriate activities, structures, and policies to ensure the most efficient and effective delivery of educational services to the Learning Society?

Responses to the issues raised vary enormously from state to state. Some adopt a hands-off stance, because they are unaware of the issues or their alternatives. Others take a laissez-faire approach either to avoid controversy or to implement the choices of a free market. Most, however, seem to be striving for coordination and cooperation among providers. Policies and practices range from encouraging cooperation by collecting and disseminating information and convening meetings for providers to creating new cooperative structures or designating existing providers as coordinators. The few more intrusive state intervention policies usually involve setting boundaries—geographical, fiscal, or market.

It is clear that the number and variety of providers of educational services for adults are growing, as is the blurring of function between providers. Almost all states are making conscientious efforts to promote local cooperation and collaboration. Increased moves toward centralized statewide mechanisms to provide control may ultimately prove self-defeating in a vast system where the states' authority is unclear and where providers are marching to different drummers and reporting to a wide variety of authorities.

- What is the state's obligation to encourage "educational have-nots" to participate in lifelong learning?
- As institutions begin to seek out the adult market, what is the state's responsibility to ensure that minority groups receive equal opportunities and attention?

The Lifelong Learning Act of 1976 states that "American society should have as a goal the availability of appropriate opportunities for lifelong learning for all its citizens without regard to restrictions of previous education or training, sex, age, handicapping condition, social or ethnic background, or economic circumstance" (U.S. Department of Health, Education, and Welfare 1978, p. C-1). Most states also have some type of statement in their planning documents that makes equal access to education a high priority. Indeed, among the 44 planning documents relevant to lifelong learning reviewed by Cross (1978), recommendations for ensuring access to appropriate educational opportunity predominated. Although it would appear that today quality may have replaced access as the issue of top priority, access nevertheless remains a major concern of state and federal policy makers.

This chapter attempts to answer three questions that appear to concern state and institutional policy makers. First, what is the present situation with respect to the participation of adults in adult education? (The answers to this question will naturally vary by state, but most states reflect the national situation, and national data are used in this section.) Second, what are the barriers to participation in adult education? Third, what are current approaches to extending educational opportunities to adults?

Participation in Adult Education
The U.S. adult population is considerably better educated than it was only a few decades ago. High school completion rates rose from 50 percent in 1950 to 75 percent in 1962, and today 85 percent of the 25-year-olds nationwide have completed four years of high school (U.S. Bureau of the Census 1982). While high school completion rates for minorities do not yet equal those of whites (see Astin 1982, p. 175), the education gap between young whites and young blacks has been closing. The largest educational

gaps now exist, not between those of different races, sexes, or income, where recent efforts have gone to increase educational opportunity, but between different age groups. People 25 to 29 years of age are twice as likely to be high school graduates (85 percent) as people 60 years of age and older (42 percent). For minorities, the gap between generations is even greater. Seventy-four percent of blacks aged 25 to 29 have completed high school, compared with only 20 percent of blacks aged 60 to 64. For those of Spanish origin, the high school completion rates are 58 percent for those aged 25 to 29 and 20 percent for those aged 60 to 64 (U.S. Bureau of the Census 1977). Table 2 shows the high school completion rate of various age groups.

It is highly improbable that the present education gap between age groups in the United States will be closed, but as the years pass, the generation gap will narrow as younger people who have had the benefit of widespread educational opportunity begin to replace older, less well-educated adults in the population. The gap, however, between the well educated and the poorly educated will prob-

TABLE 2

PERCENT OF VARIOUS AGE GROUPS COMPLETING FOUR YEARS OF HIGH SCHOOL OR MORE

Age	Percent
14–19	21.3
20–24	83.8
25–29	85.4
30–34	81.0
35–44	73.6
45–54	64.3
55–64	56.2
65 or older	37.5

Source: U.S. Bureau of the Census 1977, p. 41.

ably continue to grow. Virtually every study undertaken to describe adult "volunteer" learners shows that the more formal education people have, the more likely they are to participate in adult education (Cross 1981). A college graduate is more than five times as likely to be participating in some form of organized instruction as a high school dropout (NCES 1982).

It is easy to understand the dynamics behind the growing gap between the well educated and the poorly educated. Almost everything a college graduate does adds to the probability of further education, while almost everything the high school dropout does militates against it. The college graduate frequently enters an employee training program or works for a company or in an occupation that is likely not only to support but also to require further education. College graduates typically belong to social and professional groups that discuss educational opportunities; spouses and friends are supportive and admiring of educational accomplishment. And those who continue in school long enough to graduate from college were usually happy and successful in school and are familiar with the procedures and people that inhabit educational institutions.

The situation is exactly the reverse for the poorly educated. They enter low-paying jobs with few educational requirements and usually no educational benefits. They consort with friends and family who know little about education and may even be hostile to it; they lack the information networks to know about opportunities and the skills to take advantage of them. Many if not most of the poorly educated had unhappy experiences in school, and nothing that has happened to them since has changed that impression.

Thus, as the opportunities—and pressures—for adult education grow, it will be primarily well-educated people with good jobs and good prospects for upward mobility who will participate. If it is correct, that prediction has implications not only for the educational gap between individuals but for that between states and regions of the country as well. The West, for example, with the highest levels of educational attainment already, is pulling farther ahead of other regions through larger numbers of adults participating in adult education (see table 3) (NCES 1982; U.S. Bureau of the Census 1977).

TABLE 3

EDUCATIONAL ATTAINMENT AND RATES OF PARTICIPATION IN ADULT EDUCATION FOR PERSONS 14 YEARS OF AGE AND OLDER, BY REGION

Region	Percentage Completing Four Years of High School and More[a]	Percentage Participating in Adult Education[b]
Northeast	60.8	10.3
North Central	61.8	13.5
South	55.5	11.2
West	67.2	17.6
Total (U.S.)	60.6	12.8

Source:
[a]U.S. Bureau of the Census, CPR, Series P-20, No. 314, December 1977, pp. 41–42.
[b]National Center for Education Statistics 1982.

The evidence suggests that adults with high levels of education are more interested in education than their less well-educated peers, that they are more articulate and effective in expressing their demands for education, and that through their participation they create a climate of acceptance for adult learning that becomes contagious. Thus, states with well-educated citizens are likely to pull ahead of states where adults' educational attainment is lower, thereby increasing economic and educational inequities between states and regions of the country.

Most of the efforts toward equal opportunity of the past two decades have been targeted, not at different age groups and the powerfully age-linked variable of educational attainment, but at women and minorities. It is clear that these policies and practices have made a difference in the educational opportunities available to young, full-time students. The situation is not as clear for part-time adult learners, but women have made far greater gains in adult education than have blacks and Hispanics.

Adult women have closed the gap between the sexes at every income level and every level of educational attain-

The more formal education people have, the more likely they are to participate in adult education.

ment. In every age group and overall, a greater percentage of women than men participate in adult education (NCES 1982). The rapid and substantial increase in women's participation in adult education since 1969 is especially noteworthy given the somewhat lower educational attainment of women and the fact that women consistently report more concern over the cost of education than men. Women are more likely to be paying for their own education, but the principal disparity occurs in employer-funded programs, where men are about twice as likely to obtain funding as women. Funding from employers is, of course, unavailable to those who are entering or reentering the labor market or are seeking education for new jobs—those more likely to be women—while funding is more readily available for those seeking promotion in present jobs—those more likely to be men. Further, employer-funded programs are more likely to be available to executives and managers (who are predominantly men) than to clerical workers (predominantly women) (Cross and Zusman 1979).

The situation is quite different for blacks and Hispanics. At every age level for both men and women, the participation of blacks and Hispanics in part-time adult education is about half that for whites (NCES 1982). Between 1969 and 1975, the participation rate in adult education for whites increased from 10.2 percent to 11.7 percent to 12.1 percent. In contrast, the participation rates of blacks showed a consistent *decrease*, from 7.8 percent to 7.4 percent to 6.9 percent.[2]

The apparent widening of the gap between blacks and whites in adult education is puzzling. It fails to hold up in some analyses, and a positive interpretation could be put on it if one assumed that the greater availability of financial aid for blacks between 1969 and 1975 resulted in a shift out of part-time adult education into full-time college study. A carefully controlled statistical analysis of data from the 1975 NCES triennial survey found that blackness and/or low family income in and of themselves have little direct effect on participation (Anderson and Darkenwald 1979). The severe underrepresentation of these groups in adult

[2]While data for 1981 show a rise in participation to 13.8 percent for whites and 7.5 percent for blacks, the survey definitions and procedures used for this information were sufficiently different to render comparisons of trends of dubious value.

education is due largely to other factors associated with poverty, especially low educational attainment. The question of whether race per se is a deterrent to participation in adult education needs further study, especially by age group and educational background.

Barriers to Participation in Adult Education
Because it is usually the people who "need" education most who fail to participate in voluntary adult education, understanding the barriers to participation has been a subject of special interest to educational researchers and policy makers. Unfortunately, it is usually even harder to find out why people do not do something than why they do.

Although asking people what prevents them from doing something it is presumed they would like to do has many problems, that method has been the most common approach to identifying the barriers to participation. The barriers that people identify, usually from checklists presented to them on questionnaires or in interviews, can be classified under three headings: situational, institutional, and dispositional. *Situational barriers* are those arising from one's situation in life at a given time. Lack of time because of responsibilities on the job or at home, for example, deters large numbers of potential learners aged 25 to 45. Lack of money deters young people and other low-income individuals; lack of child care deters young parents. *Institutional barriers* consist of all those practices and procedures that exclude or discourage working adults from participating in educational activities—inconvenient schedules or locations, full-time fees for part-time study, inappropriate courses of study, for example. *Dispositional barriers* relate to people's attitudes and perceptions of themselves as learners. Many older citizens, for example, feel that they are too old to learn. Adults with poor educational backgrounds frequently lack interest in learning or confidence in their ability to learn. The data in table 4 reflect barriers that people feel are "important in keeping [them] from learning what [they] want to learn" (Carp, Peterson, and Roelfs 1974).

The motivation for adult learning is inevitably complex and consists of a combination of variables (see Cross 1981, Ch. 4, 5, and 6, for research, theory, and a model for analyzing the barriers to participation). States, however, have

TABLE 4

PERCEIVED BARRIERS TO LEARNING

Barriers	Percent of Potential Learners[a]
Situational barriers	
Cost, including tuition, books, child care, and so on	53
Not enough time	46
Home responsibilities	32
Job responsibilities	28
No child care	11
No transportation	8
No place to study or practice	7
Friends or family don't like the idea	3
Institutional barriers	
Don't want to go to school full time	35
Amount of time required to complete program	21
Courses aren't scheduled when I can attend	16
No information about offerings	16
Strict attendance requirements	15
Courses I want don't seem to be available	12
Too much red tape in getting enrolled	10
Don't meet requirements to begin program	6
No way to get credit or a degree	5
Dispositional barriers	
Afraid that I'm too old to begin	17
Low grades in past, not confident of my ability	12
Not enough energy and stamina	9
Don't enjoy studying	9
Tired of school, tired of classrooms	6
Don't know what to learn or what it would lead to	5
Hesitate to seem too ambitious	3

[a]Potential learners are those who indicated a desire to learn but who are not currently engaged in organized instruction.

Source: Cross 1981, p. 99.

a limited number of options for lowering the barriers. The most common statewide approaches to increasing access to educational opportunities for adult part-time learners are offering special programs for targeted subpopulations perceived to "need" education, making information available about existing opportunities, adjusting costs for students, and taking education to learners in isolated or underserved areas through technological means. The remainder of this chapter presents a general picture of what the states are doing in these four areas.

Targeted Subpopulations

The particular populations that are targeted for special attention in adult education vary enormously state by state. Some states are especially interested in programs for the elderly, others for particular minority groups, still others for non-English-speaking refugees. This section concentrates on three groups common to many states—adult illiterates and functional illiterates, non-English-speaking adults, and the elderly.

In almost all states, adults with limited communication skills present a clear and unambiguous priority. One in five adults, 23 million Americans, lack the abilities in reading, writing, and computation needed to handle the minimal demands of daily living, and an additional 34 million are able to function but not proficiently (Hunter and Harmon 1979, p. 27). Increasingly, states are taking action to make sure that students graduating from high school are not functionally illiterate. Thirty states require eighth grade skills in reading and writing to qualify for a high school diploma (Hunter and Harmon 1979, p. 25). The goal, of course, is to reach young people before they become illiterate adults, but in the meantime, out-of-school adults still must be reached. Recent figures show substantial increases in enrollments in adult basic and secondary education. Over 2 million adults participated in these programs in 1980, a 14 percent increase over each of the previous two years (NCES 1981).

The majority (81 percent) of people enrolled in adult basic and secondary education programs are less than 45 years old and looking for work; 45 percent are enrolled in the basic level (grades 1 to 8), 26 percent in secondary-level programs (grades 9 to 12), and 28 percent in ungraded programs, which are usually designed for people of limited English-speaking ability. Statistics vary enormously among states; nearly half of all adults in basic and secondary education programs are in four states: Florida, California, Texas, and New York. Not surprisingly, California, Florida, and Texas combined enroll two-thirds of the Hispanic participants; the District of Columbia, Georgia, Mississippi, and South Carolina enroll more blacks than whites; and Florida enrolls more than half of the participants 65 or older (NCES 1981).

The question that is surfacing now in many states is not whether attention and support should be given to adult basic skills but where the primary responsibility should lie to reduce overlap and competition yet make access to basic educational opportunity available to adults throughout the state.

In many states, the community colleges, with their commitment to open admissions and adult part-time learners, have developed extensive remedial programs for adults. Doing so, however, has sometimes brought them into direct competition with programs offered by local school districts. In California, both community colleges and local school districts have responsibilities for adult education, but the primary responsibility for adult education involving non-collegiate-level work is assigned by statute to the school districts. The assignment is more complicated than it looks, however. Community college districts may offer adult basic education and courses leading to a high school diploma if mutual agreement exists between high schools and unified school districts and community colleges. Through this process of mutual agreement, seven community college districts do have responsibility for adult education in their jurisdiction—including high school diploma programs, occupational training programs, adult continuing education, and remedial education.

In Illinois, community colleges have provided the majority of elementary and high school completion programs, although in some regions of the state, high schools have assumed responsibility. Legislation created local planning districts for adult basic and secondary education congruent with existing community college district boundaries and required that planning documents agreeable to both high schools and community colleges in the district be submitted to the State Board of Education before funds would be provided (Wallhaus and Rock 1983).

In Florida, the Adult General Education Act of 1981 specifies that all adults must have the opportunity to acquire the basic skills necessary to function effectively in society, and considerable effort has gone into establishing both local (by community college district) and statewide coordinating councils and advisory groups (Bing 1982, p. 8). In general, the state's role in ensuring access to adult basic education and high school completion programs has been to create financial incentives and to encourage (increasingly to require) local resolution of local disputes.

A second target group, adults with limited English, has received renewed attention with the influx of immigrants from Indochina and Latin America. Nationwide, the growth in classes for non-English-speaking adults has nearly tripled, from 206,400 in 1977 to 577,400 in 1980. Much of this growth can be attributed to California, which enrolls 36 percent of all adults in this program (NCES 1981).

The variety of educational services needed for recent immigrant groups runs the gamut from basic education to bilingual education to the documentation of education and experience of well-educated immigrants. The New Jersey Statewide Testing and Assessment Center, for example, helped Cuban professionals who had left Cuba without documentation verifying their education or experience establish their qualifications (Simosko 1983).

A third target subgroup has received very little attention to date by either state or federal government, but with the aging of the U.S. population and with better health and increasing longevity, the elderly are beginning to receive modest attention, most of it in the form of tuition waivers to colleges and universities (Romaniuk 1982). The elderly are among the least well-educated subpopulations in the United States; despite substantial recent gains, they also are quite unlikely to be participating in any form of adult or continuing education. In 1981, only 8 percent of those 55 to 64 years of age and only 3 percent of those 65 and older participated in any form of organized adult learning. No subpopulation recognized in the NCES data tabulations had lower rates of participation than adults over the age of 65, except adults with 0 to 8 years of schooling (which would include large numbers of the elderly) (NCES 1983). These figures contrast starkly to the recommendations from the past two White House Conferences on Aging. In 1971, the conference stated that "education is a basic right of all age groups. It is continuous and henceforth one of the ways of enabling older people to have a full and meaningful life, and as a means of helping them develop their potential resource for the betterment of society" (p. 6). The 1981 White House Conference on Aging reiterated that education for older people is not only a right but a necessity.

Initiatives for doing something about access to educational opportunity for the elderly seem to have started with institutions rather than with state or federal policy. In 1979, roughly one-third of all institutions of higher education waived or reduced tuition for older people. One-half of them had adopted such policies before the implementation of statewide policies, and 274 institutions indicated that their policy existed before the 1971 White House Conference on Aging (Romaniuk 1982, p. 7).

Most states adopted policies regarding older adult learners in the mid-1970s, either through legislation or through action by the appropriate governing board (Romaniuk 1982). Most states waived tuition and allowed older people to take regular courses for credit, usually, however, only when space was available. Some states have policies permitting students whose fees have been waived to be counted into the total determination of full-time equivalent (FTE) students, thus providing an incentive for institutions to develop programs to attract older learners. In other cases, older students whose fees have been waived cannot be counted toward FTE enrollments, even if they are registered for regular credit courses. In states where this policy is in effect, the institution bears 100 percent of the cost associated with the attendance of older learners—a significant disincentive to developing appropriate programs for the elderly.

The assumption underlying the policy to waive fees is that older people have the desire and ability to participate in college classes but lack the money to do so (Romaniuk 1982). Research does not demonstrate the validity of this assumption, however. Indeed, college classes are among the least favored learning opportunities mentioned by the elderly, and cost is actually more likely to be mentioned as a barrier to education by young people than by older people (Cross 1981). So why do states offer this particular policy as their major option for access for the elderly? Perhaps "the most cogent, covert explanation for why such state policies became popular was that they appeared to be giving senior citizens an outstanding benefit, while costing the state little or nothing in return"(Romaniuk 1982, p. 16). Despite the rather dubious motivation, the question remains: Do the programs appear to be meeting the need—or perhaps a need—of older learners? "After almost ten years, during which U.S. postsecondary educational institutions have adopted, on a wide scale, tuition-waiver plans for senior citizens, embarrassingly little is known about the diverse programs scattered among 43 states" (Long 1980, p. 140).

Based on the available research, however, very few elderly people, relative to their numbers in the population, participate in these fee-waiver programs—typically fewer than 1 percent—and those who do participate are above average in educational background and income. It is unclear whether these programs would be continued if they were more successful, i.e., if large numbers of the elderly began to take advantage of them. No state with large numbers of people over 60 (Florida, California, New York) has an FTE reimbursement plan, which would encourage institutions to attract older learners (Romaniuk 1982, p. 58).

While it seems clear that tuition waivers are not an adequate response to the educational needs of the growing population of elderly citizens, even those programs are in jeopardy because it is the institutions that are supporting and underwriting most of the costs for administering programs for older adults. Without some additional incentives, it seems highly unlikely that colleges and universities will expand their efforts or do anything very creative in the way of developing programs for this target group. (See Romaniuk 1982 for an excellent discussion of the issues involved in devising programs for the elderly from the perspective of both potential learners and potential providers.)

The identification of subgroups of adults needing special attention is probably the most realistic way to reach the hard-to-reach adult, but such programs are expensive. They require "total push" efforts, including dedicated staffing, energetic recruiting, locations accessible by the target group, and special counseling and support programs. Given budgetary realities in most states, the big question is how to assign priorities among the possible target groups that could benefit from education. Although it is likely that most states are plagued by the problem of competing demands from the advocates of a variety of population subgroups, no solution, partial solution, or even constructive way to address the problem is apparent. Yet it is painfully clear that without state incentives and intervention, the gap between the poorly educated and the well educated will continue to grow. In hard times, especially, educators will direct their programs to affluent, easy-to-reach, and easy-to-teach adults. Access for disadvantaged subgroups will simply not occur in a laissez-faire or free-market approach to adult education.

Providing Information about Adult Educational Opportunities

The provision of information about adult learning opportunities has been called the "missing link" in adult education (Cross 1978; New York State Education Department 1981). Research suggests that the major need in adult education is not more opportunities but a better system of linking potential learners to already existing options (Peterson and Hefferlin 1975). In recognition of this fact, the 1976 Amendments to the Higher Education Act authorized a three-year program of Educational Information Centers. The centers were to be state-level efforts to deliver information and guidance to adults. Although the federal program authorized $90 million total for the three years, the program was never funded at more than $3.5 million in any of the three years of its existence. When that amount was divided among 50 states, it amounted to little more than seed money. That seed money did, however, manage to start a number of states on the path to designing information systems. Providing information about adult education opportunities, however, has slipped since the 1970s and is fairly low on most state agendas today. States *should* be involved for a number of reasons, however (Hilton 1983).

First, states need information about who is providing what to whom for their own coordination and planning. Demands for new programs, competition among providers, waste and overlap cannot be addressed without accurate, up-to-date information on the educational resources of the state. Once collected, the resources cannot be efficiently used without some way of connecting potential learners with the available opportunities.

Second, most provider-sponsored outreach activities tend to be "provider-centered" rather than "learner-centered." The information is provided as advertising to attract new customers rather than to inform potential consumers of their alternatives.

Third, state intervention is probably essential for social equity. Left to themselves, entrepreneurial providers (which include colleges and universities these days) will target both their programs and their informational efforts to paying, motivated customers who tend to be well-educated people with good jobs. Doing so will most certainly increase the educational gap between the haves and the have-nots.

Fourth, well-informed consumers are probably the most effective force on providers to offer quality programs at reasonable cost. "Regulation" is going to be virtually impossible in the face of the vast diversity of providers of adult education.

Fifth, states can take advantage of certain economies of scale in the collection and dissemination of extensive amounts of information. Moreover, with the increasing use of technology, distance delivery mechanisms, and external degrees, purely local information systems will not provide complete information on which to make decisions.

Sixth, some coordination of format is essential if adults are to be able to compare and to select the alternatives that are best for them.

These reasons for state *involvement* do not necessarily imply that the state needs to be the direct provider of the services. Educational brokering services linking potential students to providers already exist in most states. Many of them are local, community-based counseling services that derive their basic funding from federal, state, local, or foundation grants. They may be based in schools or colleges, in libraries, in social service agencies, or even in industry. The New York Telephone Company, for example, with funding from FIPSE, trained eight educational advisors whose services are in such great demand that an appointment must be made 2½ months in advance (McGarraghy and Reilly 1981). This situation is not very desirable, but it suggests that the need is there. Experience with employer-based information and advisory services both here and in Europe suggests that the workplace is a good place to reach adults who are not well served by traditional education. The majority of employees served by New York Telephone Company advisors, for example, are nonmanagerial women.

In New York, a Kellogg Foundation grant has helped to expand educational and career information centers based in libraries. Libraries have long served as both the repositories and retrievers of information. Their neutral image and their extensive system of branch libraries located in neighborhoods make them a frequently overlooked natural for providing information about educational and career opportunities.

In Oregon, the Career Information Service is organized as a center at the University of Oregon's School of Community Service and Public Affairs, but the computers that make the information available to adults can be found in schools and colleges, libraries, and shopping centers. An Oregon study found that two-thirds of the adults who experimented with the computer were willing to pay $5.00 or more to use it, a user fee that would support the cost (Oregon Educational Coordinating Commission 1976). The two most complete brokerage services are likely to be clustered at the extremes of the humanistic/technological continuum of individualized services. At the humanistic end are a substantial number of small community-based organizations with volunteer help and meager funding whose expertise lies more in their personalized counseling and advocacy for educationally disadvantaged adults than in their collection and retrieval of current information about the options. Some evidence suggests that these people-oriented services are more effective with poorly educated adults than are either printed directories of educational options or computerized information centers (Cross 1978).

At the other end of the spectrum are the interactive computer guidance systems such as SIGI (System of Interactive Guidance and Information), developed by Educational Testing Service, and DISCOVER, available from American College Testing Program. Both SIGI and DISCOVER use the computer to help the user explore values, interests, and skills and to match them with career and educational options. Versions of SIGI and DISCOVER are currently being developed that are specifically for adults, the latter incorporating earlier software of the Council on the Assessment of Experiential Learning called ENCORE, which helps learners inventory their prior learning and learn how it can be converted to college credit.

The most interesting variation on the theme of providing information to adult learners is New York's "Plan to Learn" public awareness campaign. The campaign is a comprehensive program to make New York residents aware of the importance of adult learning, the extent of present participation, and the variety, quality, and accessibility of learning opportunities in the state. The governor's office proclaimed Adult Learning Week, and press and public service announcements, adult learning fairs, local organizations, etc., will attempt to convince adults that learning is fun and a legitimate adult activity and that age, previous education, geography, handicaps, and finances are not barriers to learning (New York State Education Department 1982).

The workplace is a good place to reach adults who are not well served by traditional education.

An encouraging number of creative initiatives have appeared from a great variety of sources with respect to providing information about adult learning. If a trend is apparent in all this variety, it seems to be toward computerized systems to provide information, bolstered by human counselors providing outreach and advocacy.

One of the advantages that states should be looking for in the computerized systems is feedback from potential students about their educational needs. In the 1970s, almost every state conducted a statewide "needs assessment" to try to determine adults' needs and desires. Typically, they were one-shot surveys that all too frequently collected and disseminated data without ever implementing the findings (Cross 1983). It should be possible to provide continuous feedback from computer users that would be potentially more useful in planning adult education than the occasional "study" of adult educational needs.

The dissemination of information about a state's educational resources is critical to planning, use, efficiency, opportunity, and ultimately quality assurance. But if access for underserved populations is to be a priority, far more information is needed than we now have about which dissemination methods reach which populations and how recipients turn information into action.

Student Costs
Participation in adult education is associated with annual family income. In 1981, only 6 percent of the population with family incomes under $7,500 participated in organized adult educational activities, while almost 19 percent of those with family incomes over $50,000 did so (NCES 1983). Further, the percentage increased steadily as level of family income increased.

States that wish to improve access to low-income groups may conclude that the cost of taking adult education courses may be acting as a barrier to participation. Underrepresentation by low-income groups is more complex than such a simple answer, but costs are a factor amenable to state policy. Little research has compared costs to students of various adult learning services, although the charge for any one type of education can vary enormously from state to state.

No state intentionally singles out adult students to pay higher prices for their education and training. Many policies and programs do have the effect of discriminating against part-time students or people who did not acquire certain skills in the traditional age sequence, however.

Some of the disparities in cost between full-time and part-time students are based on conscious policy choices by state decision makers—based, for instance, on the belief that part-time learners are probably working full-time and therefore can afford to pay more. But more often than not they are simply extensions of financial policy enacted before the adult learning movement blossomed. Few states have comprehensively tackled the difficult questions raised by the issue of pricing policy for adult learners:

- What kinds of adult learning are considered to have "social benefits" and therefore are worthy of state subsidy?
- What criteria should be used to distinguish between what states will and will not subsidize—location of the course? time of day offered? course content? student outcomes?

- Are certain categories of adult learning more appropriately supported by federal and local governments? What if federal and local support does not stretch to fit the demand?
- Should states concentrate cost benefits on those groups previously not well represented in adult education or simply let those who are most interested receive support?
- Can educational prices serve as a kind of "screening device" for how sincere adults are about furthering their education and training?

State policy makers do address many of these questions when making decisions about program and course subsidies, tuition, and financial aid programs. States could also choose to reduce the costs of education to adults through vouchers or employer and individual incentives.

Program and course subsidies
The most important decisions states make that affect students' costs are determining what will be fully, partially, or not at all subsidized by public funds. State government subsidies are determined by a number of variables, such as credit and noncredit hours, on-campus or off-campus students and activities, and availability of external support (Jonsen 1978, p. 363).

No two states subsidize adult learning in the same way, although some generalizations are possible. For instance, most states supplement federal and local funds in areas of English as a Second Language, high school equivalency, and adult basic education so that costs to students are minimal (Bing 1982). Most states heavily subsidize vocational job training at public institutions. On the other hand, continuing education for professionals is rarely subsidized by state funds as it "directly enhances the earning power of presently employed individuals" and often "the private sector will invest in this kind of education" (Pickens 1980, p. 11). Finally, most states expect learners to pick up the costs of avocational/recreational courses.

One issue that complicates comparisons between states and even within a single state is how certain terms are defined. The meanings of "credit" versus "noncredit" and "off-campus" versus "on-campus" often cause such controversy within a state that definitions must be spelled out in state law or administrative code. And what may be agreed to as the definition in one sector of postsecondary education does not necessarily work for another. "The broad scope of the community college mission may make the distinction between credit and noncredit less sharp than it is at the four-year level" (Jonsen 1978, p. 364). In addition, the broad geographic service area lines usually drawn around community colleges may mean there is no real distinction made about what is offered "off-campus."

Some states have attempted to look beyond such general terms to determine what is worthy of subsidy. A review of state planning documents and education statutes reveals a fascinating array of criteria that states have chosen to help make finer distinctions. They range from course location, time of day offered, and time it takes to complete the course to the subject or purpose of the course.

For example, in a 1974 report on adult and continuing education, a Texas task force approached the issue from a philosophical standpoint of what are reasonable expectations of adult learners.

> *A compelling reason [exists] for having continuing education students pay for a significant portion of the cost of their instruction—program success and relevance are greatly enhanced, if not ensured, by having the participant pay for what he or she is learning. Adults, it has been concluded, do not pay for education which is not relevant to their needs or not of a quality to meet their objectives. It is considered essential, therefore, that public continuing education programs be supported partially by student tuition fees* (Coordinating Board 1974, p. 18).

What is unusual about this example is that Texas approached the issue from the standpoint of what is appropriate for adults to pay rather than what the state should be subsidizing. Of course, once having decided that some contribution from adult learners is appropriate, the more difficult question of how much that contribution should cover arises.

Oregon chose to use place of instruction as a criterion for subsidy. State law was amended in 1978 to define continuing education as "limited to instruction scheduled to be held at least 30 miles beyond the campus of the 4-year institution offering such instruction" (Oregon Revised Statutes, Section 348, 450, (2)). This law had the effect of limiting state support of continuing education offered by four-year institutions to that offered within 30 miles of a campus.

The Arizona legislature made statutory changes in 1981 to allow subsidies for some courses offered in a time sequence different from most courses. Community colleges can now receive state funding for "open entry–open exit" vocational courses, defined as "those vocational and technical education classes which commence at various times throughout the year" (Education Commission of the States 1981). Presumably, this means lower costs to students, because they typically would be paying for instruction in less time than a full semester or a year.

In Maryland's community college system, priorities have been established for what is eligible for state funding, what might be eligible, and what is not eligible. Courses in vocational-technical education, industrial training, developmental education, community development, and health and safety education all receive state subsidies. Courses in another group receive funding only after review by the State Board for Community Colleges. They include courses that "fulfill supplemental, certification, licensure or relicensure educational requirements for professionals within the community college's service area, when they provide learning opportunities for the elderly, and when they provide educational and training opportunities for the handicapped" (Maryland State Board for Community Colleges 1978, p. 3).

Some states have attempted to look beyond course titles to the purpose of the course to determine eligibility for state subsidy. This issue is one of the more complex ones for state policy boards, because it can involve trying to determine students' motivation for taking the course, student outcomes, and "rigor" of coursework and assessment.

The state of Nebraska made such an attempt in its *1978 Goals and Recommendations for Adult and Continuing Education Instructional Programs*. The legislature charged the Nebraska Coordinating Commission for Postsecondary

Education with arriving at "clear identification of adult and continuing education responsibilities between elementary-secondary level and postsecondary level to prevent duplication of effort" (p. 1). The Commission identified five major forms of adult and continuing education, where they were being offered, and the revenue source associated with each program (see table 5).

Graphic display of this information made it clear to the Commission that "delivery systems and funding sources overlap between levels of adult and continuing education" (p. 24). Based on the legislative directive, the Commission report went on to recommend delineation of responsibility in the various forms and defined their meaning, objectives, and delivery system. The Commission arrived at an "ideal scheme" of who would offer what forms and how they would be financed. These recommendations included (1) eliminating local subsidy for avocational-recreational courses at secondary, two-year postsecondary, and graduate levels; (2) taking four-year postsecondary institutions out of adult basic education altogether; (3) increasing tuition (and hence decreasing government subsidy) for vocational education at secondary and two-year postsecondary institutions; and (4) increasing the proportion of costs picked up by tuition for degree-credit education in four-year and graduate institutions.

Probably the most regressive approach to determining what is worthy of state subsidy is when states base funding on the time of day courses are offered. In several states, evening and weekend instruction—much of it identical to daytime programs—is not eligible for state support, which has the obvious effect of having working adults pay full cost for what is heavily subsidized for younger, full-time students. A report from the Minnesota Higher Education Coordinating Board (1981) explains the historical reasoning behind this approach and why it believes that policy should be changed.

The separate funding status of Continuing Education and Extension is a legacy of a time when the public did not expect postsecondary institutions to devote serious efforts to serving the entire adult population. It was a time when formal education was restricted to youth, and further education had connotations of serving the cul-

TABLE 5

FUNDING OF ADULT AND CONTINUING EDUCATION, BY LEVEL OF INSTITUTION, PROGRAM, AND SOURCE

Source of Funding

Instructional Programs of Adult and Continuing Education	Secondary				Two-year Postsecondary				Four-year Postsecondary				Graduate Postsecondary			
	Federal	State	Local	Tuition	Federal	State	Local	Tuition	Federal	State	Local	Tuition	Federal	State	Local	Tuition
Adult basic education	X		Y		X		Y		X*	Y*						
Avocational-recreational education			Y*	X			Y*	X	Z	Z	Z	Y¹		Y*		X
Vocational-occupational education	Z	Z	Z	Y*	Y	Z	Z	Y*	Z	Z	Z	Y		Z		Y*
Degree-credit education						Z	Z	Z		X		Y*		X		Y
Continuing professional education													Z	Y		Z

1 = Cooperative extension courses
X = Major funding (more than 60 percent)
Y = Minor funding (less than 15 percent)
Z = Relatively equal funding (within a 10 percent range)
* = Changes recommended

Source: Nebraska Coordinating Commission for Postsecondary Education 1978.

tural interests of the leisured classes. While Continuing Education and Extension provides educational enrichment to the general public, it also has developed into an important means of access for adults who are acquiring their basic undergraduate and graduate education. If these aims are worth supporting, public policy should be neutral in funding delivery at different times and places . . . (p. 6).

Similarly, Massachusetts public colleges and universities run generally lucrative divisions of continuing and graduate education, which offer degree programs in the evening and which by law are not eligible for state support. This policy financially penalizes adults who have work or family responsibilities during the day, because the cost of a three-credit course in a Massachusetts state college is $75 for a part-time student during the day and $135 in the evening. Over the course of an entire undergraduate degree program, this difference would add up to costing an evening student $7,200 more than a day student!

One final criterion that might be used for determining state subsidy has been suggested by the California Community Colleges Board of Governors. In 1982, the state legislature directed the board to develop a contingency fee plan in the event that revenue shortfalls in fiscal 1984 would require that tuition be charged for the first time. Believing that those pursuing their first college degree should continue to receive tuition-free community college education, the board adopted a novel plan that would charge tuition "just to those students who have completed a degree or a certain number of credits" or who were not enrolled as matriculating students (California Community Colleges 1982).

These few examples from the states indicate the complex issues involved in determining what is worthy of state subsidy and to what extent. States that have looked beyond such simple classifications as credit and noncredit, on-campus or off-campus, seem to have a better chance of setting equitable charges based on learning needs rather than on personal circumstances.

Tuition
If costs influence adults' participation, then states can opt for low- or no-tuition policies to reduce that barrier. Cali-

fornia has defended its no-tuition policy at community colleges on the grounds that it improves access for low-income groups. Other states as well strive to keep tuition low at community colleges, which are the primary providers of adult education. Policy makers continually debate the balance between keeping tuitions low enough to encourage access while having students who can afford to pay share part of the cost for their education. It is generally agreed that a no-tuition policy is an extremely expensive way to improve access. In fact, all states now charge tuition at public colleges and universities.

When states choose to raise tuition, they often couple it with increased financial aid monies to not unduly hurt low-income students. This solution is not satisfactory for adult, part-time learners, however, because they typically are ineligible for aid. For needy adults, "it would be preferable to devise methods for dealing with these special cases that would not require low tuition for everyone"—perhaps some modifications in financial needs analysis systems and giving greater discretion to financial aid officers to make selective tuition waivers (Breneman and Nelson 1981, p. 109).

Many states also seek to maintain a tuition differential between their community colleges and four-year colleges and universities. A greater percent of low-income students do attend community colleges, but it is not clear that they necessarily choose to do so because they have compared prices. Greater participation in community colleges by low-income adults may have more to do with open admissions, flexible admissions and registration procedures, geographic convenience, instructional offerings, and available support services.

Some states have attempted to formulate tuition policy based on agreement about what level of support is appropriate and reasonable to expect from public and from individual support. A few states base tuition charges on a percentage of the cost of instruction. Students in four-year colleges and universities are generally expected to pay a higher percentage of the cost of instruction so as to maintain the desired tuition differential between segments. In most states, however, tuition charges have become more of an annual political football. Tuition is raised to cover the gap between the cost of running the higher education enterprise and the amount the state is willing to chip in from general fund revenues.

Finally, it appears that, by and large, it is more expensive to obtain a degree as a part-time student than as a full-time student at any type of college or university. Per-unit tuition costs generally average out to be higher for part-time than for full-time students. This disparity would not be enormous, but it does add to the extra costs of being an adult student. States seeking to offset pending declines in enrollment with increased part-time adult students may wish to reconsider such disparities.

Financial aid programs

A survey of state agency heads and campus leaders in 10 states found that "inadequate financial aid for adult students was recognized by many respondents as the major impediment to fully serving the adult learner" (Bing 1982, p. vi).

Most states restrict their student financial aid programs to students carrying at least a half-time credit load. But many states have confronted the issue of "the appropriate limits on publicly supported student aid for adult learners, given the need to establish priorities for the allocation of scarce resources to different groups of aid seekers" (New York State Education Department 1981–82a, p. 8).

Part-time students are now eligible for several federal financial aid programs, although the enrollment patterns and needs analysis systems reduce the participation of many nontraditional students (Breneman and Nelson 1981, p. 153). This federal aid may relieve some of the pressure on state officials to come up with assistance for part-time students. At least 17 states do offer some financial assistance to part-time students (see Education Commission of the States 1981, 1982).

Many state tuition waiver programs reduce educational costs for adults who meet special qualifications. In Wisconsin, for instance, handicapped and disadvantaged students in adult basic education and high school programs are exempt from payment of tuition (Bing 1982). Many states waive tuition for members of the National Guard, and other groups (Vietnam veterans, displaced homemakers, law enforcement officers, and members of particular professions) also are beneficiaries of state tuition assistance programs.

Financial aid can mean a significant reduction in the cost of obtaining a degree for an adult student. As many adult learners are not enrolled in degree programs, however, extending state financial aid funds to part-time students will not affect their out-of-pocket costs.

Vouchers

State governments presumably could choose to offer educational entitlements or vouchers to adults. These direct awards might be restricted to specific types of learning or to a particular category of learners (Kurland, Purga, and Hilton 1982, p. 37). A state may determine, for instance, that adults lacking high school equivalency skills should be entitled to the necessary instruction to gain those basic skills, or a state might also decide that all residents are entitled to two years of free postsecondary education. The choice of when and where would be up to the student. Group vouchers might be awarded to adults laid off when their place of employment closed or moved out of state; they might then choose collectively to purchase new skill training from an eligible provider.

In considering any entitlement or voucher program, state officials would have to address possible limits on the purpose for which awards could be used, possible restrictions on eligible providers and types of programs, and whether only certain categories of adults should receive vouchers and entitlements. This last issue raises the important question of whether entitlements would make adult learning services more attractive to groups not well represented in adult education now. "Provision of lifelong learning entitlements might be the only way of assuring equity in the provision of subsidies for lifelong learning. A publicly provided entitlement could be allocated among the different social classes, racial groups, sexes, and so on to reflect the special needs of those groups in a way that corresponds to social notions of fairness" (Levin 1978, p. 342).

No state currently uses entitlements or vouchers to encourage adults to take courses or to help reduce their educational costs. And initiatives to use such mechanisms to provide elementary and secondary education have thus far

"Inadequate financial aid . . . was recognized . . . as the major impediment to fully serving the adult learner."

been unsuccessful. They should not be overlooked in discussions on how to finance adult learning, however.

Employer and tax incentives
States could reduce educational costs to adults through employer incentives and individual incentive policies. A good deal of education and training is already offered free to adults by their employers. But states could encourage more of the practice. Tax laws could be rewritten, for example, to allow businesses to deduct expenses incurred in employee education and training programs, particularly tuition assistance programs. Tax incentives could be given to businesses that retrain workers from obsolete jobs to new skills within the same firm.

Several states now allow community colleges, and increasingly other types of institutions, to sell their educational services to businesses at full cost. Colleges arrange to teach courses specified by the business in the time, place, and format most convenient to employees. Some colleges that have gone after this market aggressively have found it to be a highly lucrative enterprise (*California Higher Education* 1983). For state officials, contract education is not without its headaches, however. Controversies may arise over who should determine appropriate charges and whether any of the earned revenue over expenses should be counted against state appropriations.

Only a few states have used individual income tax deductions and credits to help defray educational expenses. Current federal tax law allows deductions for those persons engaged in education to maintain or improve skills needed in their current job. This is one federal policy that seems to benefit part-time rather than full-time learners. Those who attend school full time usually intend to change jobs or study a new field to switch careers. Adults employed full time and working on a degree part time can more easily prove how their studies are related to their jobs.

Some states, such as New York, let parents of college students deduct part of tuition payments and offer income tax deferments on savings later to be used to support a dependent's education. States could consider extending such benefits to adult learners. Finally, if states decide not to extend financial aid programs to less-than-half-time students, they might consider tuition tax credits up to some specified limit for payment of tuition in eligible institutions (Kurland, Purga, and Hilton 1982, p. 37).

In conclusion, state policies on students' costs seem more the result of accident or tradition than of any reasoned attempt to devise equitable and efficient pricing policies. It is hard to defend charges that depend more on when or where a student attends than on whether the learning benefits the public or only the individual. Many institutions hope to increase enrollments of adult students as the number of traditional students shrinks, so now may be an opportune time for states to examine whether their policies and programs restrict access to adult learners through inequitable costs.

Distance Education through Communications Technologies
A final approach to improving access for adults is to use telecommunications technologies "to provide teaching facilities to those who would not otherwise have access to them" (Office of Technology Assessment 1982, p. 82).[3] Numerous postsecondary education providers are using three major forms of telecommunications technology:

- audio (radio, telephone, audio conferencing)
- video (open broadcast television, cable television, satellite television, videotape microwave, and video-teleconferencing)
- computer (computer-based instruction, computer-based instructional management) (Lewis 1983, p. 30).

For several reasons, the so-called "distance learning" approaches continue to grow in popularity. They "tend to enjoy a lower per-student cost than classroom or community-based programs, and adult learners appreciate the flexibility of instructing themselves at a time and place convenient to their schedule" (Richardson 1980, p. 2).

The discussion in this section is limited to states' involvement in distance learning, the issues raised by those approaches, and examples of how some states have re-

[3]Examples in this section are extracted from comprehensive descriptions of telecommunications projects in Lewis (1983) and Office of Technology Assessment (1982). Lewis also provides addresses where readers can write for more information on many programs mentioned here.

sponded to those issues. State legislatures and higher education agencies appear to be involved at three levels: (1) no involvement or financial support; (2) the provision of services to help support institutional activities but still no financial assistance; and (3) a statewide or state-level commitment to development and use of at least one of those technologies by providing funding, leadership, and support services to the state's colleges and universities.

No state involvement

Many providers of distance learning are going about their business neither hampered nor supported by the state. State officials may be uninterested in the delivery of distance education, may lack the expertise to become involved, may feel no pressure from institutions or learners to take an active role, or may believe that other means of support are more appropriate than state intervention.

One pervasive support mechanism devised by institutions without involving state agencies is the consortium (Purdy 1980). Institutions wishing to share costs, information, resources, and administrative apparatus can join one or more of the many consortia organized around geographic areas (the North Central [States] Telecommunications Consortium, for example), by type of institution (American Association of Community and Junior Colleges Instructional Telecommunications Consortium), by subject matter (the American Bar Association's Consortium for Professional Education), by type of technology (Cable Advisory Board for Learning and Education), or by intended audience (Association for Media-Based Continuing Education for Engineers).

A growing number of national consortia provide (or intend to provide) educational services to adult learners. The following examples illustrate the extent to which adults have been identified and targeted as a potential learning market.

- The Adult Learning Service of the Public Broadcasting Service will provide all necessary assistance to help a college join with its local public television station to offer credit, noncredit, and professional and career education to adults.

- Extended Uses for Television and Radio Productions, sponsored jointly by the Coalition of Adult Education Organizations and the National University Continuing Education Association, hopes to expand on the potential of existing television and radio productions for delivering informal adult learning.
- National University Consortium for Telecommunications in Teaching has established a structured, convenient course of study leading to the bachelor's degree.
- National University Teleconference Network, founded by the continuing education divisions of 68 institutions, intends to establish a national network for teleconferencing via satellite.

Clearly, one option for states is to encourage institutions to join the growing numbers of consortia working and planning for the delivery of distance education via telecommunications.

Support services
Even if a state does not financially support distance learning, the state's higher education agency can provide services that enhance the possibilities for educational applications of telecommunications. These services can be viewed as part of the ongoing planning and research, coordination, and governmental relations functions of most state boards.

Several states have recognized the need to develop statewide, coordinated approaches for implementing and accessing rapid developments in communications technology (*Telescan* September/October 1982). The Utah Board of Regents, for example, appointed a master planning task force to make recommendations for a state multiple-option telecommunications system (Bing 1982, p. 47). Occasionally, such recommendations result in legislative proposals for funding distance learning projects.

As campuses begin to make greater use of new delivery systems, state agencies will wish to collect data and monitor developments about their use. State agencies concerned with access can attempt to assess the match between adults' needs and available technologies, what types of adults are benefitting from distance delivery, and the cost-effectiveness and educational outcomes of these approaches. Having such knowledge at hand can better inform state officials as they are involved in planning and policy making.

State boards coordinate and arbitrate between educational providers. In 1982, for instance, the Connecticut legislature directed the Board of Higher Education and the State Board of Education to establish a joint committee to coordinate the efficient use of technologies. They are to work with the state Library Board and Connecticut Public Television to develop a long-range plan for investment in telecommunications and data processing (Education Commission of the States 1982). In Rhode Island, the Postsecondary Education Commission established a coordinating body called the Rhode Island Higher Education Television Council, through which all public and independent colleges and universities and private career schools are expected to cooperate as they develop telecourses and public service programming for statewide distribution through cable television companies (Education Commission of the States 1982).

State agencies can also arbitrate disputes between or about providers. After much concern had been expressed over how to accredit and license telecommunication services that crossed state boundaries, the organization of directors of state higher education agencies (SHEEO) is helping address the issue. SHEEO and the Council on Postsecondary Accreditation received a federal grant to find ways within the regional and specialized accrediting associations and state authorizing agencies to deal with "eliminating unnecessary barriers while preserving the critical elements of consumer protection and quality assurance" (*Telescan* September/October 1982, p. 4).

States may also find themselves involved in disputes among their own institutions. Teachers at two traditional campuses in Coast Community College District (California) recently protested that telecourses offered through innovative Coastline Community College are academically substandard, which has prompted review by both four-year systems in the state (California State University and the University of California) as to whether the courses should continue to be accepted for academic credit. As these issues arise, state agencies may increasingly find themselves called on to assess the quality of distance learning.

Officials of state higher education agencies are often called upon to represent educational institutions on statewide boards, such as the public broadcasting commission, and before the governor and legislature. One role state agencies might play before licensing bodies that are allocating space on new cable TV franchises is to serve as a source of expertise and advocacy for local educators who wish to argue before the licensing board that certain space be set aside for educational purposes (Goldstein 1981, p. 42). Some state boards may be in a position to advocate legislative appropriations for distance delivery in institutional budgets. The New York State Department of Education took one such step when it proposed that legislation allowing the Commissioner of Education to establish special conversion formulas for distance learning as part of student aid to public schools be extended to adult programs (Bing 1982, p. 33). States can also conduct campaigns to inform the public of courses available for credit through distance education.

State agencies can improve the quality of distance learning offered by institutions by sponsoring initiatives that support that learning. For instance, lack of good library resources for distance learners is often mentioned as a problem. The New York Regents hope to gain legislative approval for a series of proposals that would tie participating libraries more closely together through bibliographic data bases and information retrieval systems. The Education Commission of the States suggests that states offer tax incentives to business, industry, and others for donations of funds, equipment, or technical services to promote use of telecommunications technologies (McClure 1983, p. 5). Policy makers should delve more deeply into the present educational incentive structure if they are interested in creating more efficient delivery systems. "This incentive structure [with fixed faculty, physical plant, and maintenance costs] explains why telecommunications systems have been used to extend traditional higher education rather than transform it; [and] why costs of technology have always been additive rather than allowing technology to substitute for labor [costs]" (Tucker 1982, p. 4).

As costs rise and "issues grow more complex, [higher education decision makers] will have to have available to them considerable expertise in the area of telecommunications policy and procurement" (Tucker 1982, p. 19). Issues surrounding distance learning are relevant to all state program areas (budgeting, academic, planning, information systems), so whether state agencies choose to become directly involved in the delivery of distance education or not, they may well need to develop such expertise to better perform research, coordination, and governmental relations.

Direct support

A few states have chosen to become directly involved in distance delivery of educational programs. Some of the statewide projects are aimed primarily at on-campus learners, but reaching adults off-campus is at least a secondary service market for all these projects. The one characteristic tying these projects together is that they owe their existence to state legislative appropriations.

The Indiana Higher Education Telecommunications System (IHETS) is the only statewide telecommunications system used solely for higher education. Distance delivery services focus on the continuing education of professionals, including media personnel, engineers, pharmacists, educators, and government employees. In 1980–81, IHETS began offering telecourses for undergraduate credit. The legislature appropriates money annually to IHETS, which is administered by Indiana University on behalf of all 74 colleges and learning centers in the state. While regular on-campus classes may be most students' first preference, an increasing proportion of adult learners want the convenience offered by television courses delivered to their homes.

The Kentucky Council on Higher Education also took leadership in this area by forming the Telecommunications Consortium in 1978. Undergraduate, graduate, and continuing education courses are broadcast statewide by the Kentucky Educational Television, which provides free air time to the consortium. The consortium is administered by the Council on Higher Education, which supports member institutions by providing such services as publicity, telecourse leasing, research, and faculty workshops.

The state of Alaska has been called a "forerunner in educational information technology" (Office of Technology Assessment 1982, p. 227) because of its extensive use of telecommunications to extend education across long distances. After extensive investment in technology for communications, the state added an educational component in 1977 with broadcast of daytime instructional television programs by satellite. In 1980, the state appropriated $8.6 million to implement an instructional television and audio conferencing system known as the LEARN/Alaska Network. The network is managed by the University of Alaska Instructional Telecommunications Consortium and broadcasts nearly 18 hours of programming per day for audiences ranging from preschool through adult. Despite its growing popularity, problems both unique to Alaska (five different time zones in the state) and ubiquitous (local cable TV operators that perceive unfair competition with private industry) are reported.

One example of a major state commitment to distance learning is the University of Wisconsin–Extension's Instructional Communications System (ICS). ICS is an umbrella unit for three major interactive teleconference networks—the largest telephone-based educational delivery system in the country. Each semester, over 150 courses are offered, primarily in professional continuing education and public service. Because of the nature of its noncredit offerings, over 36,000 people a year take part in ICS programs. The system is supported through general fund appropriations and programming revenue.

Several other states serve as primary financial supporters of telecommunications projects but not directly from state appropriations. Several statewide governing boards have chosen to budget part of their legislative appropriation to sponsor consortiums for distance delivery.

The Kansas Regents Continuing Education Network—TELENET—is one such example. The network offers primarily noncredit continuing education for professionals and is administered by the Division of Continuing Education at Kansas State University. All six regents' institutions contribute to programming and operation of the network. Many of the courses are specifically designed to meet requirements of continuing education mandated by state law. TELENET also offers graduate and undergraduate credit courses. By joint agreement, each institution accepts credit for TELENET courses sponsored by each of the other regents' institutions. This system offers a unique approach to *program* access for Kansas residents; because each institution sponsors at least one program not available at the other five institutions, courses in these programs are prime candidates for TELENET.

Other states that support distance learning through institutional efforts and consortia include Florida, Iowa, West Virginia, and Maryland. In Maryland, the state appropriates to the Maryland Center for Public Broadcasting part of the budget to operate the Maryland College of the Air. Other revenue is raised by the per-student enrollment fees paid to the center by the 19 participating colleges and universities.

Issues raised by distance learning

Those involved with distance learning report numerous issues that inevitably must be confronted: faculty resistance, high start-up costs, the availability of appropriate software, access to prime air time, ongoing financial support, little control over federal regulations and decisions made in the private sector. But because few states have chosen to operate distance delivery systems directly, most of these operational issues will best be left for resolution at the campus level. State officials may instead be faced with the policy issues that arise from educational applications of communications technology. Whether states fund distance learning directly or not, they can expect eventually to have to address issues of finance, equity, and quality.

Apparently no state has integrated ongoing support for distance learners with annual institutional appropriations. Most states continue to fund institutions based on enrollments, and distance learning simply requires something other than full-time equivalent students as a proxy for cost, because development costs are much higher than traditional delivery but once developed can be much more cost-effective. Attendance patterns and support services required by the two approaches are not comparable.

As noted, some states have addressed this issue by making distance delivery systems a separate budget item (Kentucky, Indiana) or by approving the expenditure of funds within a system budget (Kansas, West Virginia). Some statewide projects have received initial funding from federal funding agencies (largely FIPSE and the National Institute of Education) and hope to survive after the grant expires by user fees and state support.

Because distance learning is relatively new, it is almost impossible for state decision makers to know what is appropriate for funding. For instance, much federal, foundation, and state support was given to the development of television courses. Now it appears that providers have found it much less expensive to lease at least some programs from each other and from national producers such as the Public Broadcasting Service. Other states are reluctant to invest in a specific telecommunications technology while the industry is still in flux. And in some states, an element of dubiousness may be present among some policy makers, who suspect that institutions are grabbing desperately at new gimmicks to bolster declining enrollments. With all such qualms that accompany educational reform, it is little wonder that most statewide distance delivery to date is in relatively low-cost continuing education, not offered for credit.

Distance delivery certainly means improved access to educational opportunity by time of day and place of learning. It is not clear that it means improved access by type of learner, however. An Alaskan educator with considerable experience in distance delivery believes that "the policy questions must be more clearly viewed as access for what purposes, to what information, by whom, and under what circumstances" (Metty 1983, p. 28). In fact, "electronic media are serving primarily individuals who are predisposed to pursue further education because of their previous educational background" (Lewis 1983, p. 62). A typical enrollee is a white female aged 25 to 40 who graduated from high school, attended college for a time, and has a family income over $15,000.

Few statewide projects thus far are directed toward improving access for those with low incomes and low educational attainment. (Two notable exceptions are Wisconsin's Technical College of the Air and a state network of cable programs in New York, both aimed at adults in need of high school equivalency instruction.) "As a whole . . . the postsecondary education community is not fully exploiting the capacities of electronic media to change existing patterns of adult participation in education" (Lewis 1983,

p. 62). Most programs continue to exclude other traditionally underrepresented populations (the handicapped, minority language groups, older ádults), and access to many of the new technologies is increasingly tied to the learner's economic status (Lewis 1983).

No examples of quality control or monitoring at the state level are apparent. New delivery systems are usually subjected to far greater scrutiny locally than traditional programming, which is likely to be the case with distance delivery via telecommunications technology. States that fund these systems may well find themselves more heavily involved in the regulation of these programs as they become a larger item in the budget.

State agencies of higher education are in a particularly advantageous position in distance education through telecommunications. By familiarizing themselves with the technologies and what they have to offer to education, state officials can become advocates for acceptance and advancement of these systems. But as "neutral parties" to the actual delivery of services, they can look with a critical eye at who is being served by the technologies and how well. Much remains unknown about the delivery capacities and limitations of the various technologies and their cost-effectiveness. State agencies can help institutions and policy makers think through these issues to provide a framework for further development of distance learning. "It will pay to think now about where they make sense and where they do not, and why. A different kind of planning is called for, one that makes room for new entrants and new technologies, where that serves the public interest, and at the same time preserves what is best in the current system, where that is most appropriate" (Tucker 1982, pp. 20–21).

QUALITY ASSURANCE

- What types of quality assurance mechanisms are appropriate for what types of providers?
- Should quality assurance take into account the personal responsibility adults have for making their own decisions and accepting the consequences?
- Will market forces alone act to combat fraudulent practices?
- Are there ways short of regulation for states to help protect their citizens?
- What does "ensuring quality" mean in regard to adult learning services?
- What are the respective roles of states and accrediting associations in ensuring quality?

For some years now, the quality of degree programs for adults has been a matter of concern. In 1977, researchers from the Center for Research and Development in Higher Education at the University of California in Berkeley studied nontraditional programs for adults:

Should states assume some responsibility for "consumer protection" in [adult] education?

> *Of all the problems and issues discussed in our interviews, none received more attention and concern than those relating to program quality and effectiveness. Indeed, we were struck by what appeared to be a sense of urgency at all levels—institutional, state, and federal— for mechanisms, criteria, and procedures to assess and assure the quality of nontraditional degree education* (Bowen, Edelstein, and Medsker 1979, p. 106).

The mechanisms, criteria, and procedures for assessing quality are not easily devised, but accrediting agencies, states, and institutions themselves have made considerable progress over the past few years. So far, almost all of the attention to quality in adult programming has gone to programs or procedures that resulted in degree credit. Degree programs, however, are just the tip of the iceberg in adult education. Questions are now being raised about whether noncredit programs, especially those supported by public funds, should be subject to some type of review and quality assurance. Even if the education offered is not publicly funded, should states assume some responsibility for "consumer protection" in education, or should they assume that adults are responsible for making their own decisions about where to spend their time and their money? If a free-market policy is followed, is it reasonable to hope that "good" programs will drive out "bad"? Can adults be educated to be wise consumers so that the proliferation of regulations and restrictions is unnecessary?

The questions about quality in adult education are rising far faster than the answers. In fact, it appears that the farther state agencies advance into issues of quality in adult education, the more questions they uncover. Worse than uncovering difficult questions, however, is the prospect of doing nothing to assure quality in adult education.

A comprehensive long-range plan for quality control in adult education is found in "New York State Goals for Adult Learning Services" (New York State Education Department 1981). It is as yet a *plan*, however, that New York hopes to implement by the year 2000. The basic tenet of the plan's goal number 6, "Quality Control in 2000," is that quality will be obtained by "creating better informed citizens and strengthening consumer protection arrangements" (p. 9). Consistent with this precept is the allocation of shared responsibility for quality among adult learners, the Board of Regents and the State Education Department, providers, and voluntary accrediting and other associations. Goal 6 is an integral part of a broad set of goals that support quality from several dimensions. Goal 7, "Assessment of Learning Outcomes," for example, stresses the need for the development of assessment centers where adults may verify the results of their learning efforts. The implementation of this goal would support the assumption in Goal 6 that informed choice by consumers is an important part of quality assurance. Goal 5, "Information and Guidance Services," also supports quality in adult education by calling for information and guidance services that would make consumers aware of their options. The New York goals are appealing with respect to quality assurance because they build toward a plan that will eventually encompass all education, credit and noncredit, without having to regulate and review separately the enormous variety of programs that are appearing (see Appendix A). They do, however, assume that adults can and will become "informed consumers." At the present time, energy in most states seems to be directed more toward external review and regulation of degree programs than toward making adults informed consumers.

Since most states are currently addressing quality only in degree programs, the discussion of quality in this monograph is confined to programs and procedures that offer degrees or academic credit. They include off-campus degree programs, including those offered on military bases, and nontraditional programs, including procedures such as credit-by-examination and credit for experiential learning, that result in the granting of academic credit.

Off-Campus Degree Programs
States have probably given more attention to the proliferation and quality of off-campus degree programs than to any other single aspect of adult education. Several factors are responsible. The programs grew very rapidly, they tended to generate complaints from competing colleges, and people get more excited about quality in degree programs than in noncredit programs.

The proliferation of off-campus degree programs was especially great in the mid-1970s. A 1978 study conducted by the Carnegie Council on Policy Studies in Higher Education reported that 63 percent of all institutions of higher education were placing more emphasis on recruiting students for off-campus programs than they did in 1970 and that 65 percent expected to be doing even more by 1986. Colleges anticipating the greatest gains were those falling in the Carnegie categories of "doctorate-granting universities" and "comprehensive universities and colleges" with 92 percent and 95 percent, respectively, expecting further increases in off-campus degree programs by 1986 (Stadtman 1980).

The expansion of off-campus programs has apparently slowed somewhat in recent years, primarily because of the concern expressed by state agencies and accrediting associations over quality and quantity. Some colleges with far-flung centers are operating fewer off-campus centers than was the case a few years ago, and state review procedures in a few states have also reduced off-campus activities. In Alabama, for example, off-campus credit production decreased 70 percent between 1978 and 1981, after state review procedures were initiated (Education Commission of the States 1982).

Beginning in the mid-1970s, many states began to review off-campus programs and/or to require approval of new programs.[4] Review procedures were often hastily implemented, however. The easiest, and possibly most short-sighted, approach was to simply require that off-campus programs meet the same criteria for quality as on-campus programs. That approach had two problems. First was the failure to distinguish between nontraditional programs that were designed from the ground up for mature adult learners and programs that were "nontraditional" only with respect to location and schedule. The integrity of the truly nontraditional programs was likely to be compromised by demanding that they be small replicas of on-campus instruction. Second was the related problem that certain nontraditional procedures—for example, learning contracts, independent study—could not be evaluated by the usual on-campus process variables. Accreditation teams looking at campus programs, for example, almost always look at process variables like administration, financial resources, library resources, and student services. Even if student outcome measures are presented in the self-study, they rarely figure in accreditation procedures. The procedures used to assess nontraditional and traditional programs may be legitimately different. "Institutions predominantly traditional in character usually place primary emphasis on structure and process with less attention given to outcomes. Institutions predominantly nontraditional in character usually place primary emphasis on outcomes with less attention to structure and process" (Andrews 1978, p. 13).

It is interesting that nontraditional programs (with the notable exception of graduate level programs[5]) have generally been less subject to criticism with respect to quality than credit courses that have simply been moved off cam-

[4]State authorities contemplating the adoption of policies for review and approval of off-campus and nontraditional degree programs might profitably read two documents issued by the Council on Postsecondary Accreditation (COPA). The first is the summary of an 18-month study started in 1977 with $95,000 from the Kellogg Foundation to devise some recommendations for the assessment of nontraditional education (Andrews 1978). The second is a policy statement on off-campus credit programs adopted by COPA in April 1983.

[5]A large and generally emotional literature exists on the pros and cons of nontraditional doctoral programs, which is beyond the scope of this monograph. See Jacobs and Allen (1982) for a good discussion of these issues, especially Knapp, pp. 43–63. See also *Phi Delta Kappan,* November 1978 and April 1979.

pus. Two reasons are apparent. The first is that the designers of nontraditional programs have frequently been innovative and dedicated people who have a philosophy about education for adults and are eager to design a program with integrity and quality that offers adults different and, in their opinion, more appropriate learning experiences than those available to 18- to 24-year-olds. The second is that the easiest programs to launch are off-campus programs, which to the naive seem only a matter of seeking new locations to tap new markets. It is these programs, assumed to be off-campus replicas of on-campus services, that have resulted in charges of inferior quality.

The literature abounds with discussion of "process" versus "outcome" assessments (see, for example, Craven 1980; Folger 1977; Marcus, Leone, and Goldberg 1983; Stauffer 1981), and many contend that the problem would be solved if all assessments were outcome-oriented. The problem is that outcome measures are still in a primitive state of development, and it is difficult to assess degree programs, on or off campus, with outcome measures alone. Moreover, "factors such as faculty, library, resources, and others can reasonably be assumed to have a direct influence on the performance of students" (Petersen 1981, p. 57).

The accrediting associations, which have given more serious attention to issues of quality in off-campus and nontraditional education than anyone else, suggest that a common procedure for assessing quality can span the full range of degree programs for adults. Andrews (1978), author of a three-year study of nontraditional programs, contends that postsecondary education should be viewed as a continuum, with the traditional institutions or programs at one end and the nontraditional at the other end. While the *mix* of outcome/process variables used in the assessment of traditional programs would differ from those used for nontraditional programs, the procedures would be common. Andrews recommends movement toward a "process-performance model" to accommodate both traditional and nontraditional programs in the same accreditation model.

This position now seems central among authorities on quality assessment, with most pressing for the development of better outcome measures for both on-campus and off-campus programs. "Unfortunately, on most campuses assessing outcomes has not been tried and found difficult: rather, it has been found difficult and seldom tried" (Kirkwood 1981, p. 65).

State Actions

States have taken a variety of actions in the past two years to ensure the quality of off-campus programs:

- In Alabama, after the Commission on Higher Education was granted statutory review and approval authority for off-campus programs, the State Board of Education challenged the authority of the commission to review off-campus operations in two-year institutions. The Commission's authority was upheld by the court, however.
- The Ohio Board of Regents requires prior approval of any new off-campus programs that represent more than half the coursework toward a degree.
- In Texas, steps have been taken to strengthen the Coordinating Board's control over branch campus operations. In this case, accreditation agencies are required to conduct separate evaluations of the branch campus operations of independent institutions.
- In Virginia, all out-of-state institutions must seek the approval of the State Council of Higher Education to operate in the state. Council staff make site visits to determine compliance with state standards. Since the council began approving institutions in 1980, about a dozen sites have ceased operation, still leaving, as of January 1982, 33 out-of-state institutions operating at 51 sites in Virginia (Education Commission of the States 1981, 1982).

The Illinois Board of Higher Education has recently adopted a comprehensive policy for review and approval of off-campus programs. Because it appears representative of the type of concerns addressed by governing and coordinating boards nationwide, its major provisions with respect to quality assurance are summarized here. (The policy also addresses problems of proliferation and turf disputes; for details and special conditions, see Illinois Board of Higher Education (1983).)

The policy has three primary objectives: first, that off-campus programs be responsive to the educational needs of Illinois students, communities, and industries; second, that off-campus programs be of high quality; and third, that off-campus programs reflect the most effective use of the state's, students', and institutions' resources. The overall goal is "to strike a balance between encouraging responsiveness to educational priorities and requiring stringency and quality assurance and effective use of educational resources." The board's approval is required if a program offered at a new degree site constitutes more than 50 percent of the credit hours required for a degree. In addition, colleges and universities must annually inform the board of the number of courses offered and course enrollments by discipline and by degree level for each off-campus operation, old or new, in state or out of state. The board is authorized to review periodically all programs of public colleges and universities and to advise the appropriate governing boards if the contributions of the programs are not educationally and economically justified. In addition, the board may review the off-campus programs of independent and out-of-state institutions.

The criteria for approval are spelled out in some detail, but in general, admissions, curricula, faculty, and support services are equated to on-campus standards. Certain special provisions exist, however, for nontraditional programs (those whose design, curricular content, and/or educational objectives are not amenable to site-specific approval, those whose delivery mechanisms preclude the identification of a specific geographic location, and those delivered over telecommunications or broadcast systems that serve several sites simultaneously).

The Oregon Educational Coordinating Commission takes a somewhat different approach. It places primary responsibility for maintaining quality in off-campus programs on individual institutions, deliberately rejecting course approval or review by the commission.

There are distinct differences between on- and off-campus instructional models. The traditional on-campus model assumes a broad representation of instructional disciplines, availability of full-time scholars and faculty, opportunities for library and laboratory research and frequent opportunities for out-of-class contacts with other students and faculty members. Off-campus instruction, on the other hand, often has a limited range of course offerings, relies on part-time instructors, emphasizes practical applications, relies less on library or laboratory research and lacks the community atmosphere of the residential campus.

In addressing quality in off-campus instruction, the objective is generally to make the course content equal, not to transport all the on-campus facilities and services to an off-campus setting. Off-campus courses and degree programs can be made similar to their on-campus counterparts, but not identical with on-campus residential programs (Oregon Educational Coordinating Commission 1980, p. 4).

A number of trends are revealed in the literature:

1. States appear to be increasingly involved in the issue of quality in off-campus degree programs; actions range from issuing guidelines to conducting site reviews.
2. Efforts are increasingly made toward communication and cooperation among states, regional accrediting agencies, and institutions.
3. The approach to defining "quality" differs from state to state, but most are making their criteria more explicit. Differences are emerging in whether "quality" is what exists on campus or whether quality off campus has its own distinctive characteristics.

Programs on Military Bases
Most of what has already been said about quality assurance in off-campus degree programs applies as well to programs on military bases, but because degree programs specifically intended for military personnel constitute one of the largest postsecondary enterprises in America, this special segment of off-campus programs merits special attention. In 1978, 800,000 service men and women were enrolled part time in college- and university-level courses offered on or near military bases in the United States and around the world (Bailey 1979). Many military bases have

become major educational centers, with as many students as major universities (Millard 1983).

Some states may shrug off responsibility for college programs on military bases, reasoning that the responsibility belongs to the Department of Defense or other federal agency. A report issued by a special task force of the Education Commission of the States (1977), however, recommended that states play a strong leadership role and work with the Department of Defense and postsecondary institutions to plan and coordinate educational opportunities for military personnel."

This recommendation should be seriously considered for three reasons. First, an investigation into the quality of courses at military bases shows that quality is "shockingly uneven."

It is a potpourri of exciting fulfillments and shoddy rip-offs; rigorous standards and credit give-aways; careful supervision and no supervision; dedicated academic counselling and dreadful (or no) academic counselling; adequate academic facilities, miserable academic facilities; vigorous support from military brass, a back-of-the-hand from military brass; a fruitful articulation with military-skills training, a barren articulation with military-skills training (Bailey 1979, p. 2).

Second, it can be argued that states are in a strong position to improve the quality of programs on bases.

State agencies license or charter colleges and universities under their jurisdiction. They determine (or can by new law determine) which out-of-state institutions should be allowed to purvey educational services within the states. They have or can create bureaucratic or advisory apparatus needed to monitor on-base educational enterprises (Bailey 1979, p. 32).

Third, considerable attention has been given recently to improving the quality of programs offered on military bases, and review procedures are now being developed. A variety of organizations and people have addressed the quality of educational programs in the military, including the Education Commission of the States, the Council on

Postsecondary Accreditation, the American Association of Community and Junior Colleges, the Association of State Colleges and Universities, the Council on the Assessment of Experiential Learning, and the American Council on Education. This section briefly describes present trends and the current division of labor on ensuring quality of voluntary education on military bases.

The Council on Postsecondary Accreditation has taken major leadership in working out procedures for ensuring quality in educational programs offered on military bases by accredited colleges and universities. In 1979, at the request of the military, COPA sent teams of evaluators to 20 bases in the United States and abroad where 48 colleges were offering courses. On the basis of the case studies, the project directors developed a series of recommendations, emphasizing that the quality of programs on military bases would be considered part of the institution's total integrity and that in most respects, quality on base should be judged by the same standards and procedures as those used on campus. The language of the most recent procedures for assessing educational programs on military bases (COPA 1983b), while still insisting on comparable curricula and qualifications on campus and off for students, administrators, and faculty, is more flexible. It stresses that quality should be comparable to on-campus programs while accommodating "special needs of military students to the extent possible without compromising quality. Such accommodation may include: flexible scheduling of classes; sequencing required courses so that students may complete programs in a reasonable period of time; awarding credit for successful completion of institutional advanced standing or other approved standardized examinations, for well-documented prior learning, and for relevant military occupational specialties . . ." (p. 3). COPA also recommends appointing faculty who are "suited to teaching adult students in a nontraditional setting" and who meet "defined educational needs of military personnel" (p. 3).

COPA is also making major progress in bringing order to the various responsibilities of the regional associations. The questions are complex. Who should conduct the on-site review—the regional association where the program is offered or the regional association where the home institution is based? In the former case, regional associations would be departing from their traditional stance of accrediting institutions and moving into accrediting programs. In the latter case, all six regional associations could conceivably show up on a single base, representing institutions all across the country. In California, recent legislation requires the Western Association of Schools and Colleges to assume responsibility for accrediting off-campus programs located in the Western region, which may mean visits by WASC to programs offered by institutions accredited in some other region. The procedures adopted by COPA's Assembly of Institutional Accrediting Bodies in March 1983 smooths these problems out somewhat: "The accrediting body in whose area the military base is located shall assume primary responsibility for organizing and conducting the evaluation. Other accrediting bodies will be invited to participate in the evaluation visit when institutes accredited by them are involved" (COPA 1983b, p. 9).

The trend with respect to ensuring the quality of voluntary programs offered on military bases is clearly toward closer monitoring, increased specification of criteria for quality assessment, and greater cooperation and communication among states, institutions, and military personnel on base and in the Department of Defense. "In only a few years, the trend has changed from the 'quick and dirty' evaluative study by outside critics, which brought attention to the size, complexity and problems of this segment of postsecondary education, to the present emphasis on responsible involvement . . . " (Brown 1982, pp. 2–3).

The Department of Defense has been eager to improve the quality of on-base voluntary educational programs and issued DOD Directive 1322.8 to that end. The criteria for institutions submitting proposals now contain a heavy emphasis on approval and accreditation by civilian agencies. Directive 1322.8 calls for proposals to show evidence that the applicable accrediting body has approved the off-campus program before the program begins and to agree to be evaluated by the appropriate accrediting body during the first year of operation and at appropriate times thereafter.

Some states have been far more active than others in addressing this issue, but the usual action is to work toward better communication on the grounds that everyone—state, institutions, accrediting bodies, Department of Defense, and individual military bases—is working toward the same goal. In Florida, the State Board of Independent Colleges and Universities took early leadership and created the Advisory Council on Military Education (ACME) to facilitate communication. ACME consists of 22 members, including state, military, and institutional representatives. Interest has been shown in extending the ACME concept to other states with "a significant military presence" through regional conferences and cooperation; in fact, "a constantly increasing number of states are now operating or creating various advisory and supervisory groups relating to local military education programs" (Brown 1982, p. 2).

Nontraditional Methods
One can now earn academic credit in many ways other than, or perhaps in addition to, classroom instruction. Almost all of the new alternatives are of special benefit to adults who have the ability and maturity to develop a learning plan, who have acquired college-level skills through previous study or adult activities, and who are increasingly interested in academic credentials for upward mobility.

Although external degrees and independent study are old traditions in academe, the spurt in nontraditional procedures for awarding credit occurred in the 1970s. A Carnegie Council survey found that by 1978, 81 percent of the colleges and universities in the country awarded credit or advanced standing through the College-Level Examination Program (CLEP), which gives adults an opportunity to demonstrate on standardized examinations that they have knowledge comparable to that learned in college classes. In 1970, by contrast, only 35 percent of colleges and universities granted credit for CLEP. The story is similar for credit for experiential learning. In 1970, only 14 percent of the institutions would consider awarding credit for noncollegiate learning; by 1978, 41 percent would (Stadtman 1980).

The major nontraditional procedures for granting credit to adults who can demonstrate college-level learning are by examination, by assessment of experiential learning, and through courses taken from noncollegiate providers. It is increasingly possible to put these methods together in various combinations to earn an external degree. Indeed, as early as 1976, a national study found 54,000 adults enrolled in some 250 external degree programs in the United States (Sosdian 1978).

States are involved in these alternative routes to degrees at several levels now, and any state planning ahead for lifelong learning will have to consider quality assurance in these nontraditional procedures. New York's goal for the assessment of learning outcomes in 2000 is to give credit "only for competencies achieved, not for experience or participation in a course or other activity" (New York State Education Department 1981, p. 11). The implementation of that goal would abolish the distinction between traditional and nontraditional procedures for the award of credit and require learners to demonstrate competencies learned in the classroom as well as externally. The irony is that by 2000, we may be requiring students in on-campus courses to demonstrate that their achievement is comparable to off-campus learning, as measured by learner outcomes.

State involvement in credit-granting activities ranges from direct services (at least four states offer external degrees by examination) to monitoring the amount of credit granted by institutions competing for adult learners. This discussion is limited to quality control in the three major nontraditional procedures for granting academic credit.

Credit by examination
Granting credit to students who demonstrate on an examination that they have acquired knowledge comparable to that obtained by students in a college course is an old and widely accepted practice. Most colleges today offer students an opportunity to receive credit or advanced placement rather than repeat courses on subjects they already know.

The best-known national examination program is the College-Level Examination Program offered by the College Board. The program was specifically designed for adults, and some 125,000 tests are administered annually, with another 100,000 administered to military personnel through the military's DANTES program.

Credit by examination is a measure of student learning outcomes; it evaluates students' learning rather than course procedures. CLEP tests are constructed by college faculty members teaching in the appropriate subject field, and norms are found by administering the tests to appropriate classes on campus. Levels of difficulty are adjusted to the performance of students completing the appropriate on-campus course, but CLEP can only recommend credit; colleges make their own decisions about which tests to accept, how much credit to grant, and any necessary residence requirements. CLEP offers five general examinations: English composition, humanities, mathematics, natural sciences, and social sciences and history. Some 30 subject examinations covering material taught in the most common undergraduate courses are also given: American literature, freshman English, college algebra, introductory sociology, for example. Most of the subject examinations are designed to correspond to one-semester courses, but a few correspond to full-year or two-year courses. New York has long operated its own examination program, which is available nationwide and parallels very closely the procedures and types of examinations used in CLEP.

Few questions of quality are raised anymore about credit by examination as long as the faculty in the department concerned confirms that the test is appropriate to the credits granted. Criticism is more likely to center on whether an entire degree should be granted through the use of examinations. Can a person learning independently or putting together "pieces" of learning experiences be said to be college educated? Does not some unmeasurable but essential learning take place in interaction with fellow students and teachers? In fact, evidence shows that students who spend time in interaction with the instructor and fellow students show more personal growth than those who do not (Astin 1977; Chickering 1974). But with so many part-time and commuting students, how realistic are the ideals of the "community of scholars"? For many working adults, the choice is not between an external degree and a campus program but between an external degree and no degree.

Credit for experiential learning
The Council for the Accreditation of Experiential Learning (CAEL) distinguishes between "sponsored" and "non-sponsored" experiential learning. The former involves nonclassroom learning by enrolled students in internships, cooperative education programs, and other learning experi-

ences sponsored by the college. Nonsponsored experiential learning refers to experiences before enrollment in a college—self-directed learning, community service, and on-the-job training, for example. Because the charges of overly permissive standards are directed primarily at non-sponsored experiences and because those procedures are of greatest concern to adult learners, this discussion focuses on the assessment of nonsponsored learning.

Colleges are using one of three major procedures for awarding credit for experiential learning: (1) The student's competence is observed and compared to a predetermined standard—for example, the student can give an informative, interesting, and persuasive extemporaneous speech; (2) the student's competence is compared with the competence of others—for example, the student can give an extemporaneous speech of the same quality as that given by students at the end of a one-semester course in public speaking; (3) the student's competence is inferred from the length and breadth of the student's experience—for example, the student has given many speeches as part of job or community activities (Knapp and Jacobs 1981).

The last method, say Knapp and Jacobs, is the least desirable because learning from experience should be recognized, not the experience itself. In their survey of CAEL institutions, however, they found 42 percent of the institutions using comparison to a predetermined standard, 21 percent using comparison to the competence of others, and 37 percent using inference from a student's experience. Thus, despite the fact that CAEL's "first rule" is to award credit only on the basis of demonstrated learning, a significant number of institutions rely on inference as their dominant method, some justifying it on the grounds that experienced, full-time faculty members make the judgments.

A major problem for anyone wanting to equate learning to educational credits is the lack of a standard semester hour. On-campus credits are granted without question on the basis of two rather dubious assumptions: (1) that different students receiving three semester hours in English from different instructors have made the same amount of progress toward the goals of the college, and (2) that a student receiving three semester hours of credit in English has made the same amount of progress toward the goals of the

Can a person learning independently or putting together "pieces" of learning experiences be said to be college educated?

college as a student receiving three semester hours of credit in dance or philosophy (Knapp and Jacobs 1981). If the goal of giving credit for off-campus learning is to make it interchangeable with credit awarded for traditional classroom study, the problems are obvious and lend even more credence to New York's long-range goal of giving credit only for competencies that can be demonstrated.

A number of efforts are now being made to bring greater rigor and accountability to the granting of credit for experiential learning. Some are nationwide, such as the 300-college consortium of CAEL, some are institutional, and a few are taking on statewide colorations.

The Statewide Testing and Assessment Center at Edison State College in New Jersey was established to facilitate the awarding of college credit for adult learning regardless of where or when that learning took place. Seventeen colleges are members of the Center, whose purposes are:

1. *to enable adult students enrolled at traditional colleges earn college credit through nontraditional means and have those credits apply toward their degree programs;*
2. *to foster the development and/or expansion of institutional policies to award credit for college-level knowledge obtained outside the formal classroom;*
3. *to train college faculty to serve as assessors of students' prior learning;*
4. *to facilitate the articulation and transfer of credits among participating colleges;*
5. *to serve as a regional assessment center model* (Simosko 1983, p. 3).

Among the activities of the center has been the training of some 250 faculty members to evaluate adults' educational backgrounds (so-called "portfolio assessment"), which, under CAEL's leadership, is becoming an increasingly rigorous procedure (see, for example, Keeton 1980; Knapp 1981; MacTaggart 1983). Colleges experienced in the assessment of experiential learning find that the greatest problem now is preparing students for the process (Shipton and Steltenpohl 1981). Some colleges are now preparing students in classes or workshops where students are helped to develop portfolios of past college-level learning that link the assessment of lifelong learning to educational planning.

The advantage of New Jersey's Statewide Testing and Assessment Center is that it increases expertise, decreases the likelihood of institutions' "using" credit as a competitive recruiting device, decreases the expense of establishing multiple assessment centers, and makes it easier to disseminate information and services to students. If the assessment of learning outcomes becomes increasingly popular, which it seems to be doing, states may want to consider playing a direct role in assessment, providing incentives for institutions to form consortia, or taking other steps to make the services represent groups of institutions rather than individual colleges.

Credit for noncollegiate sponsored instruction

Increasingly, adults are requesting college credit for courses taken outside formal educational institutions, and increasingly colleges are granting credit for learning that can be demonstrated relevant to the student's degree program. Several states have developed a number of alternative routes to college credit. New York contends that "it is sound educational practice to grant academic credit for high quality educational programs conducted by noncollegiate organizations, provided that the courses are at the college level, and that the credit is appropriate to an individual's educational program" (Program on Noncollegiate Sponsored Instruction 1982, p. 1).

The surge of interest in credit for courses offered by noncollegiate providers has a number of reasons. First, some of the courses are very similar in format, content, and performance requirements to those taught on campus. Second, many noncollegiate organizations are offering extensive programs of courses at the college level, and they claim that employees are more eager to enroll and perform well if college credit is available. Third, national and statewide mechanisms now exist for assessing the quality of such courses and making credit recommendations to colleges. Fourth, adults in a competitive job market are increasingly interested in converting their learning into salable credentials.

Two major programs now exist for converting learning acquired under noncollegiate auspices into college credit.

Both are national in scope, but one is operated by New York state, the other by the American Council on Education (ACE). ACE started shortly after World War II, through its Commission on Accreditation of Service Experiences (CASE), to make credit recommendations for courses taught in the military. In 1974, the Board of Directors of ACE expanded the role of CASE to include other alternative routes to college credit. The ACE office concerned with these matters is the Office on Educational Credit and Credentials, which exists to reduce the institutional burden of evaluating students' requests for credit while helping students enter the mainstream of postsecondary education at an appropriate level of achievement.

The history of direct credit recommendations for courses taught in business and industry and other noncollegiate providers started in January 1974 when the University of the State of New York started to evaluate courses taught by corporations in New York and to make credit recommendations for them. The first pilot study consisted of 102 courses taught in eight noncollegiate organizations. In August 1974, ACE joined New York, and for three years the program was operated jointly. In 1977, ACE withdrew to operate its own independent program, and the New York program continued under the auspices of the New York State Board of Regents. By 1983, the ACE program had become a consortium, listing the following state agencies as collaborators in the program: Consortium of the California State University and Colleges, Florida Department of Education, Illinois Board of Higher Education, Iowa Coordinating Committee for Continuing Education, Massachusetts Board of Higher Education, Michigan Board of Education, New Jersey Board of Higher Education, North Carolina Joint Committee on Transfer Students, Pennsylvania Department of Education, Tennessee Higher Education Commission, and University of Wisconsin System Consortium.

The scope and procedures of the ACE and New York programs are virtually identical. The 1982 catalog published by the New York Program on Noncollegiate Sponsored Instruction (PONSI) contains some 1,565 courses offered by 150 organizations that have been evaluated and recommended for credit since 1974. The 1982–83 ACE publication, *The National Guide to Credit Recommenda-*

tions for Noncollegiate Courses, contains over 2,000 courses offered by 183 noncollegiate providers. Both catalogs are distributed nationwide to colleges and universities. Providers in both programs include business and industry, professional and trade associations, voluntary associations, labor unions, government agencies, hospitals, and cultural institutions. In addition, courses using new technologies are making their way into the catalogs. Control Data, for example, has established a learning center network, which offers self-taught computer-based courses in most major cities. In 1980, a special section was added to the New York catalog to accommodate courses offered under the Comprehensive Employment and Training Act.

The review process for including a course in either catalog is far more stringent than that used in the review of most college courses. When the sponsoring organization requests a review by PONSI, the following criteria are applied before an on-site evaluation is scheduled: Courses must present what is thought to be college-level material. Classroom-based courses conducted over an extended period should contain at least 30 hours of instruction; those offered on an intensive basis should be at least 35 hours in duration. Such courses must have a prescribed program of instruction and be taught by qualified instructors. All courses must include an appropriate method of evaluating students' performance. In the case of correspondence and independent study courses, a supervised final examination must be administered under secure conditions (PONSI 1982, p. 3).

In addition, the sponsoring organization must submit detailed information about the course, including a syllabus, instructional materials, evaluation procedures for measuring students' performance, criteria and procedures for selecting instructors, educational background and work experience of students taking the course, and the duration of the course.

If enough courses are to be evaluated to constitute a full day's work, a review team of approximately three faculty members is appointed to look at facilities, talk with instructors and sponsors of the course, and determine whether the course is college level. If it is, recommendations are made regarding the level (e.g., lower division baccalaureate/associate degree), subject area (e.g., electrical technology), and number of credit hours. This information and a description of the course then appear in the catalog. Credit recommendations are valid for up to 10 years from the date of the evaluation, provided the courses are not substantially changed. In addition, organizations are contacted regularly to determine what changes if any have been made in the content and structure of the courses. (ACE requires annual reports about the courses and a formal review every five years.)

The model for reviewing courses offered by noncollegiate providers is, unlike the credit by examination and credit for experiential learning, based on a process model of review, supported by outcome measures. That is, it is the course that is being evaluated rather than (or in addition to) student outcomes.

Not surprisingly, given the rigorous standards and review procedures of both the New York and ACE programs, few complaints are lodged about quality. A 1976 follow-up study showed that 68 percent of New York colleges and universities had an institutionwide or departmental policy on using the credit recommendations or were developing such a policy. A majority of the courses (82 percent) submitted by students to colleges in 1975–76 had been accepted for credit, but students were also using the credit directly for job advancements, salary increments, and professional licensure or certification (McGarraghy and Reilly 1981).

The probability is strong that noncollegiate providers who request and receive credit recommendations for their college-level courses will continue to increase and that few complaints will be lodged against the quality of these carefully reviewed·programs.

Conclusion
Although the quality of off-campus programs still needs improvement, the literature and state documents on quality in adult education lead one to believe that giant steps have been made in the past five years toward controlling the quality of adult degree programs. The question "What is quality?" appears to be straightforward and objective, when in fact it is neither. The too-simple response that appears in state documents and the literature is that "quality" is whatever exists on campuses. Significantly, those

involved most deeply and for the longest period of time in the study of the problem are somewhat more inclined to use flexible language and recognize legitimate differences in on-campus and off-campus programs than those who are just beginning to look at the problem.

> *All parties involved must be cautious not to prescribe uniformities in regulations and procedures through regional, state, military or other well-intentioned groups which could stifle experimentation, innovation, creativity and performance above a currently perceived threshold level of acceptability. Programs should be judged by the logic of their conceptualization, strength of performance, and validation of successful outcomes while remaining appropriately fluid to respond to both internal and external changing demands and conditions* (Brown 1982, p. 6).

The "urgency" felt just a few years ago has by now turned into commitment to monitor quality and confidence in the eventual outcome. The Sixth Annual Conference on Quality in Off-Campus Credit Programs hosted by Kansas State University in late 1983 had a healthy nationwide attendance, and continuing interest in the topic seems assured. Whether similar concerns will arise regarding quality of noncredit programs and consumer protection, however, remains to be seen.

- What role do state education agencies have in forecasting the labor force?
- To what extent should states attempt to retrain and redistribute workers from obsolescent fields into growing fields of economic importance to a state?
- Will the connection between a strong system of higher education and the ability to attract businesses to a state force higher education into changing program emphasis, for better or for worse?
- Should the cost of specially tailored educational programs be assumed by the state or by business and industry?

Although not specifically designed as a strategy to improve learning options for adults, the recent interest in the revitalization of the economy through development of human resources may prove to be one of the most substantial boosts to adult education of all state policies.

Agreement is widespread that we are facing a major revolution in society. The term coined by Marc Porat (1977) to title his nine-volume study on the shift from an industry-based to an information-based economy, "The Information Economy," seems to best capture the concept. In 1940, only 25 percent of the jobs in the United States involved the processing of information; today probably more than 50 percent of all workers are creating, processing, or distributing information (Porat 1977). The authors of *Global Stakes: The Future of High Technology in America* (Botkin, Dimancescu, and Stata 1982) describe the knowledge-intensive economy as a shift "from products to services, from physical resources to human resources, from investment in machinery to investment in knowledge, from capital intensity to knowledge intensity, from a domestic economy to a global economy" (p. 160).

A report issued in 1982 by the Office of Technology Assessment (OTA) of the U.S. Congress concludes that "the so-called information revolution, driven by rapid advances in communication and computer technology, is profoundly affecting American education. It is changing the nature of what needs to be learned, who needs to learn it, and how it will be provided and paid for" (OTA 1982, p. iii). For higher education, it has been called "an immense opportunity—probably the single most important opportunity we will have in this decade, and perhaps the remainder of this century" (Edgerton 1983, p. 13).

Already this new age has been felt and responded to in the educational enterprise. It can especially be seen in the responses of:

- *students,* who are increasingly choosing technology-related courses (computer science, mathematics) and job-oriented majors;
- *institutions,* which are requiring more vigorous precollege preparation in mathematics and sciences, are reallocating resources from liberal arts and humanities to more vocationally oriented curricula, and are designing novel ways to secure computers and other technological equipment for their academic programs;
- *business and industry,* which has developed extensive education and training programs for employees, has become more assertive in saying what it needs and expects from higher education graduates, and has cooperated with colleges and universities in many ways to bring it about;
- *state government officials,* particularly many governors, who believe that the resources of their higher education institutions, put to the right uses, may spell economic recovery. Their responses have ranged from comprehensive strategies linking higher education with economic revitalization to line items in state budgets to fund a job-training program.

Education and training of adults is becoming the linchpin of human resources development.

Many state programs and institutional practices arising from this movement have significant implications for adult learning. Some have intended consequences for working adults and those wishing to be employed; others are designed to provide a better climate for business and industry.

The scope of these responses is wider than the purpose of this monograph. This chapter therefore concentrates on those policies and programs directed at what has been called "human resources development." Because of the changing demographics of the workplace, education and training of adults is becoming the linchpin of human resources development. With the "baby-bust" population having reached working age, the growth rate of the American workforce is slowing dramatically. Today's workers will constitute over 90 percent of the workforce in 1990 and over 75 percent of the workforce in the year 2000. "The nation's success in renewing its economy will depend heavily on how well and at what pace *existing* workers are trained, retrained, and upgraded" (Choate 1983).

Education has long served as the training ground for the country's private sector. But never before has so much attention been focused on the role state government can play in preparing workers for business and industry. This chapter is in two parts. The first section ("State Activities") examines why state officials—particularly governors—are interested in the preparation of workers, the types of programs that are believed to aid the economy through education and training of adults, and approaches states can take to provide the private sector with an appropriately skilled labor force. The second section ("Policy Questions") addresses the link between education and a revitalized economy, presenting five issues for the reader's consideration.

State Activities

State officials' interest in the preparation of workers

Since the New Deal, jobs programs and economic development have been largely the concern of the federal government. Increasingly, however, state officials—particularly governors—seem to be making them their business. Some of the reasons for this interest include the desires to balance state budgets, reduce unemployment, and attract high-tech industry.

For a number of reasons, most states are having difficulty balancing their budgets from one year to the next. The ninth annual *Fiscal Survey of the States* calls FY 1983 "the bleakest year ever" (National Governors Association 1983). It reports that aggregate state budget balances are at a new low, dropping over $4 billion from fiscal 1982 to 1983. Five percent of total state expenditures is considered a prudent end-of-year surplus, but by the close of fiscal 1983, the 50-state balance was expected to be less than $30 million, or 0.2 percent of current expenditures (p. 1). Such conditions have meant general fiscal austerity, including across-the-board and selective program cuts, delayed expenditures, and even permanent tax increases in many states.

Few politicians appear to be waiting on a national economic recovery or an infusion of federal dollars to shore up their sagging economies; many states have decided to rely on their own resources and strategies to improve economic conditions.

One of the economic conditions most in need of attention is high unemployment. Governors in states like Washington, Michigan, and Pennsylvania are coping with double-digit unemployment because of their heavy reliance on so-called "mature industries"—lumber, automobile manufacturing, and steel. Most are aware that the reported unemployment figures are probably too low, as they do not account for the discouraged unemployed, who are no longer actively seeking jobs. So in the midst of a dramatic period of retrenchment overall, 28 states have initiated training and retraining programs for workers (Magarrell 1983b), as well as other business-oriented initiatives. For governors and legislators to be funding growth in a program area during a period of overall retrenchment indicates that they perceive some compelling societal needs, not the least of which is getting people back to work.

Many governors see the surest way to economic recovery as attracting and keeping high-tech business and industry. They perceive the shifting base of the economy and hope to make their state a leader in service and information industries, or at least to have some part in them, for two reasons. First, high-tech industries are not limited in possible location to where they have been before. (Witness the movement of many old and newer high-tech firms out of the Silicon Valley.) Second, the potential for growth in many high-tech products has not yet been exhausted. The right combination of factors may just mean that a state can become a major center for these industries.

One generally unspoken but nonetheless sobering side of these initiatives is that states are competing against each other for what is probably a relatively limited resource. A.G.W. Biddle, president of the Computer and Communications Industry Association, estimates that high-technology industries have a significant presence in only nine states (Pollack 1983). Even in California, pioneer state of the silicon industries, high technology is expected to account for only one out of every 14 jobs in the state by 1990. State policy makers should be aware that tying new education and training support to programs designed to boost high-tech industries may be undermining both their own economic base and their educational system.

Many governors have in fact chosen to think more broadly than high technology to revitalize their state's economy. A review of fiscal 1983 budget proposals from the nation's governors indicates a number of other strategies involving education: improved support for the infrastructure, extraeducational enterprises, programmatic support, comprehensive strategies, and education and training programs.

Some governors stress the need to restore earlier cuts that may have weakened the overall system of higher education. In proposing his budget for the State of Washington, which included increased support for faculty, equipment, and research, Governor John Spellman characterized it as recognizing "the critical role that higher education must play in our economic recovery and expansion" (Magarrell 1983a, p. 12). Another governor called for a tax increase to prevent the erosion of education.

At least five governors have proposed establishing centers to promote research in science and technology programs (Maryland, North Carolina, Florida, Indiana, and Connecticut). Other proposals include facilities and support to "incubate" innovative industries.

Many governors earmarked funds for growth in specific program areas, most typically business, computer science, and engineering (Missouri, New Mexico, California). While support in these areas can easily be justified, this kind of "categorical" funding may have a serious defect. State officials will need to consider whether an institution is capable of nurturing an excellent engineering school, for instance, while the rest of the college's programs are crumbling around it for lack of support.

A few governors—in conjunction with other state officials—have adopted the attitude that the transformation of their economy must be approached in something other than a piecemeal fashion. Ohio is notable for higher education leadership's playing an integral part in shaping economic transformation. The Ohio Board of Regents laid the groundwork in its 1982 *Master Plan for Higher Education* by outlining how higher education could forge a "new social compact" with business, with the ultimate goal of advancing the quality of life in Ohio (Ohio Board of Regents 1982b).

Support for education and training programs is largely directed at community colleges. Both specific training programs and general increases in support for technical and skill training have appeared in proposed budgets (North Carolina, Maryland, New Mexico, California).

Types of programs

In helping their states prepare for the information economy, state officials have directed money and attention primarily to two areas of postsecondary education: job skill training, usually at community colleges, and improvements in undergraduate mathematics, science, and engineering programs. Although some adults will benefit from improvements in undergraduate programs, discussion here focuses on training programs. Graduate and continuing professional education is also discussed, although few states have initiated programs for adults in these areas.

Job training. Most new state support for skill training is going toward programs that respond to the recent technological advances in electronics (not only in electronics-related industries but also in fields where production processes are being substantially altered by the application of computers to the industry) and programs to retrain displaced workers into fields with labor shortages.

Community colleges are often chosen to supply the educational component of state-sponsored retraining programs. Their geographic dispersement, their history of responding to local industrial needs, and their curricular emphasis on vocational education make them the logical center for adult retraining programs. In California, the community colleges benefit from the California Worksite Education and Training Act (CWETA) program. The state awards grants to community college districts, which work in cooperation with local business and industry to provide entry-level training or upgrade skills in vital areas. For example, the Los Angeles Community College District offered a training program for employees at Fairchild Control Systems Company. This program, which involved 32 weeks of classroom instruction and 20 weeks of on-the-job training, was intended to lead to promotions for Fairchild employees in the field of CAD/CAM (Computer-Aided Design/Computer-Aided Manufacturing) ("Customized Training" 1982–83). Community colleges provide instruction in these programs, and often local businesses contribute state-of-the-art equipment.

South Carolina's Board for Technical and Comprehensive Education (TEC) initiated a program to improve the resources and instruction available to teachers and industrial personnel in electronics-related areas. TEC established the Center for Innovative Training in Microelectronics, ordered $250,000 worth of state-of-the-art electronics equipment, and hired a director and staff. The center is designed to provide training for industry through customized training courses for specific firms and training for instructors at the state's 16 technical colleges. The staff expects to train about 500 instructors and industry personnel per year in microelectronics, textiles, machine design, word processing, graphics, and other allied professions. "While serving the needs of existing firms in South Carolina, the Center is viewed by Governor Riley, officials at the State Development Board and TEC officials as an attraction for high technology industries to South Carolina" (Tri-County Technical College 1982, p. 4).

The commonwealth of Massachusetts is not as concerned with attracting high-tech industries as it is with ensuring that it can continue to provide existing firms with an adequate supply of skilled labor. In response to this need, the state legislature in 1981 set up the Bay State Skills Corporation to encourage industry and higher education institutions to develop short-term training programs in high-growth fields. In essence, businesses that need workers trained in a specific field match funds made available to a local college (public or private) by the state.

Two interesting aspects of Bay State Skills are that the program is not intended to provide skills to any certain group of people (for example, the long-term unemployed or youth) and that private higher education institutions are just as likely to receive state grants as are public institutions. Some may argue that public postsecondary institutions are the most appropriate place for state-sponsored job training programs, but Nolfi (1982) encourages state planners to consider "new institutional arrangements and partnerships, whereby individuals can arrange the meeting of their education and skill needs through many combinations" (p. 360).

States are also the recipients of federal money for job training programs through the Job Training Partnership Act (JTPA), which is designed to replace the earlier Comprehensive Employment and Training Act (CETA) program. Federal officials plan to give states more leeway in designing and implementing programs (*Higher Education Daily* 20 December 1982); where adult and youth training programs were separate under CETA, JTPA lets local administrators establish the mix, with the requirement that at least 40 percent of training funds be spent on youths aged 16 to 21.

State officials would certainly welcome additional support for adult training programs. Not everyone, however, agrees that retraining programs for adults provide long-term solutions to problems like structural unemployment and the need for an improved economic base. No "clear and definitive evaluation" of the impact of federal manpower programs in the 1960s and early 1970s has been performed (Feldstein 1973, p. 24), but the evaluations that have been done suggest that these programs have "positive but small effects" (p. 24; see also Davis and Morrall 1974).

Some states have taken concerted steps to retrain workers who are the victims of plant closings resulting from the relocation or failure of a business or from a business's subcontracting out part of its operations. California's "Investment in People" campaign gives grants to community colleges to help retrain workers displaced by industrial plant shutdowns. Colleges receive support based on average daily attendance and may supplement that support with federal job training and Vocational Education Act funds.

Another partnership between the federal government, the state of California, General Motors Corporation, and the United Auto Workers attempted to respond to the need for retraining 9,000 employees left jobless by GM plants' closing in northern California. If high unemployment continues, much more attention to this issue can be expected. Government officials in several states are already being pressed to make the effects of closing plants the responsibility of the businesses that choose to relocate and not the responsibility of the state and people it has left behind. (At this writing, no efforts at such legislation have been effective.) This problem, too, is a thorny one for state officials: States that pass worker-oriented legislation will have a harder time attracting new businesses to the state, but states that do not provide such protective legislation are left with the human costs of plant closings when businesses decide to pick up and move elsewhere.

Programs for displaced workers are requiring more than skill training (Lublin 1983). Retraining workers for high-demand fields may well require workers to relocate to wherever those jobs are available. Most displaced workers are middle-aged males with strong local roots and es-tablished working-class life styles. They often own a home in an economically depressed area and may be supporting their children through college. Such workers are not prime candidates for relocation programs. Because states would not typically become involved in such federal retraining and relocation programs, they must be careful to focus retraining programs for displaced workers around high-demand industries near the same location where workers were laid off. Such constraints lead one to believe that state retraining programs for displaced workers, while important, will never become major adult education pro-grams.

Displaced workers and other technology-skill training programs are efforts by states to provide technical workers to business and industry. But the need to prepare profes-sionally trained adults for the information economy raises a number of important issues for higher education.

Masters programs. Two gradual but significant changes have occurred in postbaccalaureate education over the past decade. First, masters programs are less and less exten-sions of the full-time undergraduate experience and more programs designed for and attended by working adults. Second, they are less and less training grounds for doctoral studies and more practice-oriented curricula for working professionals.

Institutions have responded to the eager market of al-ready well-educated professionals by offering an enormous variety of certificate and masters programs in locations and at times convenient to their work lives. Residents of the New England area can choose from over 350 separate mas-ters programs at public colleges and universities, by virtue of a voluntary regional student exchange program. The proliferation of practice-oriented programs caused the Ohio Board of Regents to raise the issue of what distinguishes such graduate programs from undergraduate programs. "This is especially hard to answer in masters programs designed for in-service education of working professionals. These programs frequently lack coherence around central themes and purposes" (Ohio Board of Regents 1982b, p. 18).

The relatively sudden national call for more trained professionals in mathematics and science has created certain problems for state policy makers. The approval process for new programs at public institutions—which often takes as long as three years from program idea to program start—means that private and proprietary institutions may saturate the market with graduates before a public institution can graduate any.

Some public institutions also are caught in the position of wanting to offer masters degrees in popular fields but lacking a strong enough undergraduate program in that area to support graduate-level instruction. This problem is particularly acute in fields like computer science, where the undergraduate program may well be having difficulty recruiting and retaining qualified faculty and keeping equipment current. Although most recipients of masters degrees in mathematics and science hope for new private sector jobs or promotions, a critical shortage of teachers trained in these areas remains. The commonwealth of Virginia took the initiative to help solve this shortage. The Board of Education initiated a program, with legislative approval, to retrain public school teachers as math instructors. The program is financed by a new application fee for teacher certification and is structured so that it takes no more than two summer sessions. States might also consider recruiting from another potential pool: employees in the private sector with math and science backgrounds who may be looking for a transition before retirement. The University of Vermont and the Harvard Graduate School of Education have both initiated such programs and expect to prepare for teaching positions a small number of Masters in Education graduates with significant work experience in math- and science-related fields.

State retraining programs for displaced workers, while important, will never become major adult educational programs.

Continuing professional education. The issue of what types of continuing education are needed for professionals in science, technology, and engineering is beginning to receive attention. The National Science Foundation report on *Science and Engineering Education for the 1980s and Beyond* (1980) describes the need for "field mobility" by these professionals (p. 43). Field mobility permits scientists and engineers to sense new opportunities and relieve personnel shortages in particular subfields. Continuing education programs are viewed as important in helping facilitate mobility, and they are seen as increasingly important as the pace of technological discovery increases. With the half-life of a computer scientist's knowledge estimated at five years, these professionals may always be running to catch up (Botkin, Dimancescu, and Stata 1982, p. 130).

A group of highly regarded engineers and computer scientists associated with the Massachusetts Institute of Technology suggested that the future of engineering education should be continuous throughout the working life of the engineer and that it will be provided by industry and education working in partnership (MIT 1982). The report rejects the notion that a few years of formal education can provide an adequate foundation for half a century of professional work. Moreover, the demand of the 1980s cannot be met by replacing "obsolescent" engineers with new graduates, even if that were a humanly acceptable plan. Thus, they conclude, "the only apparent alternative is better utilization of the presently available engineering workforce through continuing education at the workplace, with the active encouragement and support of employers" (MIT 1982, p. 6).

The popularity of the tutored video instruction (TVI) methodology developed at Stanford University indicates a growing interest by engineers and other industry professionals in receiving continuing education at the worksite. TVI uses televised broadcasts of on-campus classes with audio feedback. Recordings are shipped to off-campus locations around the country, where they are played back to small groups of students led by a local tutor. This program has been operating for a decade and is cited in the MIT report as a "simple economical way of providing instruction" (p. 38). The informal and participatory style "is likely to better fit the needs and tastes of older engineers"

(MIT 1982, p. 39). As TVI and other telecommunications programs are used by more and more firms to provide graduate and continuing education for engineers, states and their institutions may be winding down as providers of continuing education for high-tech professionals.

Approaches to supplying a skilled labor force
States can use six basic strategies in trying to mediate between the needs of business and industry and the training provided workers by postsecondary education: the free-market approach, state program approval, meeting needs specified by business, comprehensive services supplied by higher education, decentralized planning and cooperation, and the consumer-driven approach.

Free market. This approach involves little or no state planning or intervention. It is based on the kind of entrepreneurial spirit recommended to community colleges by Delaware Governor Pierre A. duPont IV: "Don't sit back and wait for government and business to come to you. Seek out meetings with key business and government leaders in your community and tell them about the training services your colleges can offer" (Parnell 1983, p. 16).

In fact, most states use the free-market approach in letting community colleges decide which vocational programs to offer. If students seem to be demanding training in an area, if the college's local industrial advisory council agrees with the need for skilled graduates in that field, and if the college staff can agree to offer the program, a proposal will be sent to the state for official approval. Such programs are rarely given serious scrutiny at the state level unless they require extensive funding or are opposed by a neighboring college or proprietary school. By the time the request for approval reaches the appropriate state official, the college is already offering numerous courses in the subject and simply needs sanction from the state to grant it certification or degree status. State higher education agencies also feel they have little better knowledge than the colleges themselves about what local industry needs.

The free-market approach seems less suited for sorting out high-technology supply and demand. Allowing every institution to offer training programs in current high-demand areas may well result in quickly overloading the market.

Many of these programs also involve the need to purchase expensive equipment, and good faculty are so hard to come by that colleges may get in bidding wars with each other to hire them. Finally, the state has an interest in monitoring institutional conformance with missions defined by statute. Allowing the free market to determine who gets what programs may encourage colleges to stray far from their intended service functions.

State program approval. This approach is most commonly used today. Most state higher education agencies have authority over institutional program approval, and demand for increased job-oriented education and training is not coming just from governors, legislators, and the business world. Few public colleges and universities are failing to respond to this priority. Requests for state approval of programs in engineering and computer science are inundating academic affairs staffs of coordinating and governing boards. Some of these requests may be arising from an institution's desire to attract traditional and adult students to offset anticipated declining enrollment. Some institutions have carefully analyzed what the future needs of local business and industry will be. But many are simply responding to the highly elastic fluctuations in students' demands. Computer courses are overenrolled, and still numerous disappointed students are turned away. Engineering, computer, and other high-tech programs long ago instituted selective standards for admission.

Sorting out students' demands for programs, institutions' desires for useful and attractive courses of study, and workers' needs presents a considerable challenge to state higher education officials. At the most basic level, they must possess some philosophy about how far to go in manipulating the supply and demand of the marketplace.

Generally, statewide boards have placed a high planning priority on increasing the budgetary support available to high demand areas through some combination of new state dollars and university reallocation. [And under unfavorable state financial circumstances,] statewide boards generally limit themselves to highlighting major shifts in enrollment and strongly encouraging greater university reallocation. Institutions cannot take these recommendations lightly, especially as they are frequently buttressed by continuing legislative and gubernatorial complaints about constituents' being denied admission to high demand programs (Floyd 1982, p. 11).

As if determining the appropriate supply of trained graduates is not enough, state higher education agencies must also have some notion of the future demand for those graduates. This requirement is fraught with difficulties, not the least of which is the need to ask business and industry to make projections of the workforce. Doing so may well result in artificially inflated figures, as it is in the private sector's interest to overstate its needs. (Any oversupply of labor allows business to recruit from a larger pool at lower prices.)

Research on the relationship between high-technology firms and educational institutions in the Boston area illustrates the difficulty. While government and industry forecasts have been projecting an increased need for a variety of skilled technicians in high-tech fields, the area employment picture is not so clear. During 1981–82, "every type of training institution—private, proprietary, CETA, and public colleges—experienced some difficulty in placing their technician graduates in jobs" (Useem 1982, p. 45). Even a small slack in hiring can make school administrators nervous, especially those of institutions that have "expanded their training significantly or are in the process of doing so" (p. 45).

Even if a state decides to arbitrate some balance between needed projected workforce and institutions' demands for programs, it is left with the politically tenuous position of saying "no" to some institutions who desire high-demand programs so as to say "yes" to others.

Most states have come to terms with these difficult issues by approving program requests when the program involves no significant new state expenditures, when the institution makes a convincing argument that it can place its graduates, when the program is not at odds with the institution's educational mission, and when state officials have no contradictory evidence that business and industry need more graduates in that field. The state is then free to initiate and fund short-term job training programs for the private sector's needs not adequately served by this process.

Meeting business-specific needs. Because the program approval process is slow and does not always result in a close match between supply and demand, a state may choose to let industry itself decide what skills it needs and then simply have educational institutions provide them. One version of this approach is being used by South Carolina's Board for Technical and Comprehensive Education. The full services of the TEC system are made available to businesses that decide to locate or expand in the state (South Carolina State Board n.d.). Through TEC's Industrial and Economic Development Division, "special schools" are established to provide short-term job-employment training programs in areas these businesses have identified. By 1983, TEC had already provided this service for 600 industries and some 71,000 people. In cooperation with company personnel, TEC staff identify levels of skills required for jobs, recruit trainees, locate instructors, and develop instructional materials. The training itself often takes place at the nearest technical college. State program directors call this highly successful program their "start-up in the black" concept.

The Bay State Skills Corporation, described earlier, is another form of letting individual firms determine what training programs will be offered. In general, this strategy is probably more suited to short-term technical skill programs than to comprehensively mediating supply and demand.

Comprehensive services from higher education. Rather than deal with these issues as part of its ongoing program approval, the Ohio Board of Regents decided to focus on the connection between the needs of business and industry and the resources of higher education. As part of the program activities under the Lifelong Learning Project, the Regents concentrated on finding "areas of interaction" between higher education and business and industry. The project had four objectives: (1) to assess the needs for education, training, and development of adults already in the workforce and the needs of private sector employers; (2) to determine ways in which these needs have been served and identify areas of need that were not currently being met; (3) to develop and pilot local, regional, and statewide activities that would enhance the cooperation between companies and colleges in the state; and (4) to evaluate these activities in terms of their implications for state policy and subsequent legislation (Moore, Settle, and Skinner 1983). What is particularly noteworthy about this approach is that Ohio began the process by honing in on the gap between adults' skills and the private sector's needs. In their haste to serve the needs of business and industry, other states might have made the mistake of initiating programs without seeing whether appropriately trained individuals are already available.

Decentralized planning and cooperation. Between the extremes of laissez faire and a comprehensive state effort lies the strategy adopted by the state of Arizona. Knowing that workforce needs must be met but not wanting to make that determination at the state level, the Arizona legislature delegated that responsibility in two metropolitan areas to the local community college. The colleges were designated as the state's providers of advanced technical and semiprofessional education and as the agents for delivery of programs for adults seeking retraining in or improvement of their current skills. The community college district is to coordinate vocational planning in its county in the determination of which occupational training programs will be conducted and by whom.

California also used local coordination in naming Regional Area Vocational Education Councils in the 1970s, although these councils became one of the early victims of Proposition 13.

This strategy seems to accomplish several goals. It gives a planning framework and orderly process to program development and approval. Determining the private sector's needs is more likely easier at the local than the state level. And it may encourage the kind of cooperation envisioned by the authors of the MIT report, *Lifelong Cooperative Education* (1982), where institutions, businesses, and other agencies can share faculty, equipment, and other resources.

The consumer-driven approach. One approach used by several European countries is worth considering: to offer money directly to adults and let them decide when and where to get training. The West German government, which was the originator of the idea, provides almost a full subsidy to every adult for up to two years of full-time training or retraining (Stringer 1980, p. 9). The advantage is that adults are given greater freedom in choosing to change careers; the problem is that educational institutions and industry are totally at the mercy of this free choice. If this were a state-administered program, problems of determining state residency could also develop.

The need for coordination
In those states that have attempted to revitalize their economies through retraining programs for adults, one thing has become very apparent: It is essential to coordinate the activities of the many agencies and institutions involved in these efforts. The Vermont Training Program was initiated for just that purpose, and the Colorado Commission on Higher Education reported working closely with the State Department of Labor and the State Board for Community Colleges and Occupational Education to encourage cooperation in the delivery of occupational services and programs. In Ohio, Governor Celeste charged the Bureau of Employment Services with "taking the lead in developing and carrying out a cohesive job training and retraining effort" (Steinbacher 1983, p. 1). Higher education officials are well advised to work closely with state employment services offices, which are usually hooked into the federally based Job Service Matching System. Without data on current job vacancies and two-year projected needs, "it is simply impossible for schools to plan effectively for training and education" (Stringer 1980, p. 6).

Besides initiating training programs to meet current needs, state officials may wish to ask longer-term questions about encouraging opportunities for retraining throughout the lifetime of adult workers. Do funding formulas allow continuing retraining or do they depend on legislative whims? Are admission policies and sequenced programs of study flexible enough to accommodate working adults? How much support should the private sector commit to programs designed for their benefit? If the kinds of training programs currently being developed to respond to economic revitalization continue to be popular, state policy makers should address these issues systematically.

The interest in revitalizing state economies has boosted the attention given to adults. And it is not surprising that many state initiatives for economic revitalization are directed at enhancing employment for adults rather than learning for adults, as much of the support for these programs has come from politicians rather than educators. "The high priority that advocates claim for lifelong learning generally has not been endorsed by state and federal officials, at least when it comes to providing public funds for such efforts. . . . Although few political leaders will openly criticize the concept of lifelong learning, their willingness to underwrite it . . . has been noticeably lacking" (Breneman and Nelson 1981, p. 165). Yet it appears that politicians are willing to support opportunities for adult learners when they are closely tied to a socially desirable end—the end in this case being economic revitalization.

Policy Questions
Elected state officials are usually concerned with what it will take to realize quick improvements in their state's economic condition. Training adults in new technological fields may attract and keep high-tech businesses; having high-tech businesses means more jobs; and having a better employment picture means more personal and business tax receipts for state coffers. If all this comes to pass, then these programs have made significant contributions. Yet by the very nature of their positions, governors and legislators have less inclination toward careful analysis of the long-term implications of these training initiatives. For all the discussion of the need for a human resources development *policy,* state leadership has often responded with crash *program* solutions, usually short-term job skill training programs.

As the information economy becomes better understood and less in need of immediate program solutions, perhaps state officials should take the opportunity to examine what is happening within our changing economy. Issues to be addressed include looking at how closely present approaches to training coincide with the new economic realities, what kinds of jobs are being created and whether they are relatively stable, and whether all groups of adults will be able to benefit from the new jobs in the information economy. Economists and manpower planners have offered some interesting—and often contradictory—responses to these issues. Through the critical evaluation of these arguments, state policy makers may be able to develop a better understanding of the world of work for which they are training their citizens.

Five issues are briefly explored here: *enhancing productivity* (Is there a clear link between training workers and job productivity?); *product life cycle theory* (What job skills are needed and at what point in specific industries?); *technology and job skills* (Will the information economy require more or less sophisticated job skills?); *dual labor markets* (Will the economy's new jobs be equally available to everyone?); and *education beyond skill training* (Are ways other than skill training available to prepare workers for the information economy?).

Enhancing productivity

One argument used to support state policies and programs for retraining workers is that investment in "human capital" will improve the nation's lagging productivity. Human capital theory first appeared in the late 1950s and early 1960s; it requires looking at what people bring to a job besides their physical presence: "the actual energy, motivation, skills and knowledge possessed by human beings, which can be harnessed over a period of time to the task of producing goods and services. It may include abilities acquired through some more or less formal system of instruction . . ." (Bowen et al. 1977, p. 362). Because people earning higher wages generally have higher levels of education, increased levels of education and training are empirically associated with productivity (Becker 1975).

By the 1970s, other economists began to take serious issue with productivity's being tied so closely to schooling. Some argue that completion of educational programs is more a screening device to find workers who will "stay with" a job than a critical variable in improving productivity. Others contend that an overeducated workforce, rather than leading to increased productivity, may in fact adversely affect workers' satisfaction, health, behavior, and performance. A study of the impact of certain types of training on labor productivity in the manufacturing sector found in-house training to be the only form of training positively associated with productivity (Medoff 1982).

For all the theories and discussion, "the upshot of this long, confusing, and frequently arcane debate is inconclusive" (Aaron 1978, p. 88), which should warn politicians and policy makers who support adult education and training programs not to count on seeing perceptible increases in workers' productivity. For "the effect of training on productivity has not, it is fair to say, been established empirically in a clear and incontrovertible manner" (Goldstein 1980, p. 43).

Product life cycle theory

Changes in the kinds of job preparation needed by the U.S. workforce can result from factors external to business and education. Witness the glut of engineers after the scaling down of the Vietnam war and the oversupply of teachers as the number of school-aged children declined. State education planners are now more cognizant of such social and economic trends in developing master plans and in reviewing and approving programs.

But state officials may be well advised to examine another, more subtle factor affecting workers' needs—the "life cycle" of products. Product life cycle theory, a pervasive concept in the marketing literature (Capon 1981, p. 1) states that "products undergo predictable changes in their production and marketing characteristics over time" (Wells 1972, pp. 5–6).

Briefly, products are thought to experience five different stages: introduction, early growth, late growth, maturity, and decline. It appears that the labor skills needed during the various stages are quite distinct. During the early stages, product research and development and frequent design changes require a greater amount of labor, relative to capital, than later when specialized machinery and techniques can be used for mass assembly of a more stable product (Wells 1972, p. 9). Skilled labor is especially critical. In the growth phases, high production volume means a shift to mass reproduction, and labor skills are less important. By the time a product reaches its mature stage, production is highly capital intensive, and workers require little or no specific training skills (see figure 1).

"The effect of training on productivity has not . . . been established empirically in a clear and incontrovertible manner."

FIGURE 1

THE RELATIVE IMPORTANCE OF VARIOUS FACTORS
IN DIFFERENT PHASES OF THE PRODUCT CYCLE

Production Factors	Product Cycle Phase		
	New	Growth	Mature
Management	2	3	1
Scientific and engineering know-how	3	2	1
Unskilled labor	1	2	3

The purpose of the blocks is simply to rank the importance of the different factors, at different stages of the product cycle. The relative areas of the rectangles are not intended to imply anything more precise.

Source: Wells 1972.

A better understanding of product life cycle may result in less tendency to speak of "the skills needed for the new technologies." Developing industries, such as biotechnology, require highly educated men and women (Watcke 1982–83, p. 30). Products that are in later growth phases, such as much of the electronics industry, may require primarily short-term training and retraining rather than degree programs. In fact, for all the attention focused on the needs of the electronics industry, it is now fundamentally a manufacturing industry (*New York Times* 27 February 1983). Presumably, educational institutions would have little to do with education and training for mature industries, because any required skills can be learned on the job in a matter of weeks.

As state officials develop policies and programs to better prepare the existing workforce for the changing needs of business and industry, they should take a careful look at where products are in their life cycles. Retraining programs in, say, computer technology may require very different skills in three years than they do today.

Technology and job skills

The new technologies are generally expected to create the need for adult training. For example, a spokesman from General Motors told the American Vocational Association that, to repair the simplest robot, a worker needs knowledge of electronics, hydraulics, and pneumatics. The next generation of robots will have "vision and speech," requiring even higher levels of knowledge for maintenance and repair (*Higher Education Daily* 7 December 1982, p. 5).

But others are looking at the kinds of jobs being created by the new technologies and seeing something quite different. The counterargument is called "job deskilling," and "in truth, no one really knows whether technology will create more interesting jobs than it destroys. Perhaps in the long run it will. But in this decade and into the next, we may be creating an expanding number of routinized jobs requiring little specific education and training" (Edgerton 1983, p. 5). Some are convinced that "past applications of technology in the workplace [and] present evidence suggest that future technologies will further simplify and routinize work tasks and reduce opportunity for worker individuality and judgment (Levin and Rumberger 1983, pp. 10–11).

Many new electronic products are being developed with "built-in diagnostics," which informs a field technician what is malfunctioning. Instead of determining what is wrong with a circuit board, for instance, the technician simply replaces the whole board. Building products for "advance maintainability," which is becoming more common, has resulted in reducing the level of skills technicians need (Useem 1982, p. 46). "Even at the professional and managerial level, work has not become more interesting and challenging; in fact, it may have become more routine" (Lynton 1982, p. 21).

We seem to be at a critical point in determining the proper role of technology in the workplace. Most would agree that technology in and of itself is not benign and that it is how the corporate world decides to use that technology that is important. People in business and industry are daily making decisions in product development and design that will have enormous impact on the kinds of skills workers will need in the future. Electronics manufacturers, for instance, do have the choice *not* to make their products self-diagnosing. They may argue that built-in diagnostics increases productivity and consumers' satisfaction, but it is also resulting in less interesting, less skilled jobs for technicians. It may also be that technology will make some jobs in any one industry more interesting while routinizing and deskilling other jobs (Kuttner 1983).

Education policy makers may not be able to influence how the new technologies are applied in the workplace. They should be aware, however, that the information economy does not necessarily mean adults will need to return to postsecondary institutions throughout their lifetimes to upgrade their job skills. In fact, it might mean less need for recurrent education, as workers can more efficiently be trained for routine jobs at the worksite.

Dual labor markets

The information economy is generating new and exciting jobs in many fields. But a growing body of evidence also suggests that it may be creating jobs at the top and the bottom of the economic ladder and fewer and fewer jobs in the middle.

> *As the economy shifts away from its traditional manufacturing base to high-technology and service industries, the share of jobs providing a middle-class standard of living is shrinking. An industrial economy employs large numbers of relatively well-paid workers. A service economy, however, employs legions of keypunchers, salesclerks, waiters, secretaries, and cashiers, and the wages for these jobs tend to be comparatively low* (Kuttner 1983, p. 60).

In fact, the U.S. Department of Labor forecasts the largest number of job openings between 1978 and 1990 in just these latter categories. While the country is expected to have increased jobs for professions like accounting (61,000) and engineers (46,500) in that period, low-wage service and clerical openings will number in the millions. An explanation of why jobs seem to be concentrating at these two extremes is offered by the dual labor market theory, which first appeared in the early 1970s (Bluestone 1968; Doeringer and Piore 1971; Edwards, Reich, and Gordon 1975; Harrison 1972; Piore 1970; Reich, Gordon, and Edwards 1973) and has since been further refined.

Briefly, the theory states that the job market is structured into two tiers: the primary labor market and the secondary labor market. In the primary market, jobs typically offer high wages, good working conditions, stable employment, and job security. Work rules are administered equitably, and workers can advance up the job ladder (Piore 1970). The primary market can be further divided according to the types of individuals in these jobs (Reich, Gordon, and Edwards 1973). "independent" primary jobs encourage and require creative problem solving and self-initiation and often have professional standards for work. Voluntary turnover is high and individual motivation and achievement are highly rewarded. "Subordinate" primary jobs are more routinized and therefore encourage personality characteristics of dependability, discipline, and responsiveness to rules and authority. Most factory and office jobs would fall into this category, with levels of education more a function of the job market than of requisite skills.

The secondary labor market is far less attractive than either level of the primary market. These jobs offer low wages, poor working conditions, few opportunities for promotion, and little variety in the range of jobs available. The rate of turnover is high.

To illustrate how the dual labor market theory might be applied to one of the "information technologies," consider the job structure of microelectronics. This industry employs a number of computer scientists and engineers, who typically have at least a bachelor's degree and earn $30,000 a year and more. But the bulk of workers in this manufacturing industry are electronics assemblers, who earn about $12,000 a year. The number of skilled technicians whose wages fall between these two extremes is surprisingly small (Kuttner 1983, p. 62).

If the job market is indeed becoming stratified, it is important for instructors in adult education to consider where in this structure retraining programs are placing their graduates and whether certain groups are historically restricted to the secondary market. In fact, white males predominate in primary jobs, and women and minorities are overrepresented in secondary jobs. In California's Silicon Valley, for instance, "40 percent of the total electronics workforce is female, but over 75 percent of the assemblers are. . . . Forty percent of female assemblers and 33 percent of male assemblers are members of ethnic minorities" (Howard 1981, p. 5).

If the prediction comes true that two-thirds of all new entrants into the American workforce will be women—and primarily adult women—then the dual labor market structure has sobering implications for educational policy makers of a liberal bent. Policy makers who favor improved opportunities for women and minorities may see one solution as being greater participation by those groups in education and retraining programs for adults. But as most economists would agree, only so many "good" jobs are available in the economy. Policies and manpower programs designed to shift groups traditionally in the secondary labor market (i.e., women, minorities) to the primary market may require either that other groups (e.g., white males, recent immigrants) take up the slack in the secondary market or that the target groups return to the secondary market with more skills than their jobs will require. Thus, college administrators should "rethink the business they are in" (Edgerton 1983, p. 7), in part because "our picture of the future must include the ominous prospect of a new and growing underclass" (p. 5).

Education beyond skill training

Current talk about the need to formulate "human resources development" policy rarely is grounded in a desire to enhance citizenship or the analytic, communication, and interpersonal skills of our citizens. Most of the current emphasis is on arming adults with job skills needed in the current market. But several arguments for education beyond skill training are being put forward.

Policy makers should look beyond short-term payoffs of investment in higher education:

One gets the sense that any activity that lacks a direct and preferably immediate connection to "economic re-

covery" is ripe for curtailment, if not elimination. . . .
The attempt to appraise every expenditure for its eco-
nomic payoff . . . can easily damage the health and dis-
rupt the internal coherence of both the teaching and
research enterprise (McPherson 1982, p. 16).

The problem in occupational planning is not the mis-
match between the new, specialized skills needed to win
jobs in emerging industries and the skills colleges teach
their students (Whitelaw 1982–83). Rather, "the problem
quite simply and overwhelmingly is with the *level of de-*
mand for labor, not the *composition of demand.* Our economy just will not grow fast enough to employ even those
who have acquired the new skills" (p. 6). This argument
serves as the foundation for many colleges that are at-
tempting to merge liberal learning with career preparation
"to aid the lifelong learning of their students" (Rehnke
1982–83, p. 2).

Several other economists suggest reasons to support
education beyond skill training. Available evidence con-
nects higher education not only with "enhanced earnings
of workers and improved technology" but also with "personal development and life enrichment . . . the preserva-
tion of the cultural heritage, the advancement of knowledge and the arts . . . and the direct satisfactions derived
from college attendance and from living in a society where
knowledge and the arts flourish" (Bowen et al. 1977, p.
447). "Increased education may enhance a worker's ability
to acquire and decode information" (Welch 1970, p. 42).
Higher education increases students' ability to "deal with
disequilibria; to respond flexibly and constructively to
change" (Schultz 1975, p. 840).

Even America's corporate officers seem to sense the
need for investment in more than skill training. The American Association for Colleges asked Russell Warren to poll
corporate executives to see what skills they considered
important for getting jobs in their companies. The skills
they chose closely match the traditional goals of general
education. Therefore, colleges should not be too quick to
replace their general education curricula with more specialized, job-oriented programs. They should think twice before expanding "professional courses in response to popularity among students" (Warren 1983).

If indeed businesses and the economy in general benefit from education outside narrow job skill training, there may be an important lesson here for advocates of lifelong learning. If jobs and careers are going to change as rapidly as many predict, the best thing education can do for adults in the long run is offer them a solid background in general education as undergraduates and encourage continual retraining in specific job skills over the rest of a lifetime.

Levin and Rumberger (1983) support this argument for a different reason. They assert that despite the current appeal for investment in high-technology programs, most jobs in the new economy will not require high levels of skill, and, therefore, "the general educational requirements for creating good citizens and productive workers are not likely to be altered significantly by high technology" (p. 12).

This argument presents a fundamental dilemma for state government and its institutions. From the perspective of long-term educational planning and the heavy investment states have already made in supporting the liberal arts and sciences, this approach is eminently defensible. But as governors volunteer to beef up the job preparation side of higher education and students' interest shifts to these areas, state education officials are hard-pressed to argue for a reliance on higher education's traditional core. The stark fact is that what might be good for economic revitalization may not be good for preserving traditional higher education.

Finally, a society that expects to undergo many of the changes predicted in the new information economy should also be aware that technical workers will not be the only group needing continual education and retraining. Those who administer government programs, those who deal with social problems, those who deliver health care, and those who educate the nation's children will also need opportunities for professional growth.

Conclusion

This summary of the five issues is not intended to provide easy answers to how we are preparing our citizens for what kind of society. Rather, it is intended to present some provocative arguments about what role education and training might play in shaping the nature of skills needed in the workplace. Educational policy makers may choose to draw one of several conclusions from the arguments presented.

First, they may choose to worry less about long-term implications of education and training policies and concentrate instead on getting people jobs by arming them with marketable skills. Unencumbered by state policies and statutory requirements, colleges would be free to assess the needs of business and industry and develop appropriate education and training programs.

Second, they may choose to believe that "education can have little impact on the kinds of jobs available" (Kuttner 1983, p. 70). Because the real problem is the supply of good jobs rather than the supply of good workers, "an emphasis on education and training will make the workforce even more frustrated than it is now" (p. 70).

Third, policy makers could choose to rely on the desires of the labor force to determine how much and what kind of training to provide. As long as workers are willing to take courses or sign up for education and training programs, then they must be perceiving some benefit from them. "Many overeducated Americans may choose to accept a sharp break between schooling and work, viewing their education as more an item of consumption than as an investment activity" (Freeman 1976, p. 24). If work is less interesting, people may look more to leisure activities, such as education, for the personal satisfaction and sense of accomplishment that jobs used to offer.

Fourth, educators may recognize that the apparent deep structural problems in the economy have no short-term solutions. They may choose to continue offering education and training programs to reduce unemployment and supply businesses with skilled workers but also to engage in concerted efforts to improve the quality of worklife. For state higher education officials, this effort might involve more closely aligning themselves with state economic development strategies. State policies can encourage the development of alternative work settings, such as worker-owned and -managed cooperatives, that allow workers to have greater say in how jobs are structured and how technology is applied to those jobs (Mackin 1983). College and university staff may choose to build upon the cooperative relationships they have developed with local businesses and industry to go beyond discussions of immediate program needs. Educators concerned about these structural problems should consider what could be learned by including workers in discussions about job training with local business leaders. For educators, the issue of retraining adults throughout their lifetimes is more than simply helping workers skip from job to job as the world changes around them. Our economy might be revitalized in the short term by providing business and industry with narrowly trained workers, but educators can strive to help make for a continually vital economy by encouraging policies and practices that allow people to grow and develop in all aspects of their lives, including the workplace.

STATE ROLES

This chapter has the dual aim of summarizing the other chapters and developing a generalized framework for thinking about the various roles that states are playing or might play in ensuring appropriate educational services for adults. The previous chapters presented information about how states are currently dealing with four major areas of concern about lifelong learning—defining appropriate roles for the multiple providers of the Learning Society, providing access to educational opportunities for adults, ensuring quality, and revitalizing the economy through education of the workforce. This chapter weaves the woof across the warp laid down in the earlier chapters. The fabric of state roles in lifelong learning is made up of the concerns to be addressed (the warp) and ways of dealing with those concerns (the woof). The conceptual framework developed in this chapter is concerned with classifying and illustrating the various ways in which states can address the issues or concerns that are surfacing as we move into the Learning Society in which most of society's people are learners and many of society's organizations are providers of educational services.

This report has not attempted to determine the most typical state reactions and concerns about lifelong learning. Rather, the goal has been to determine the range of possible responses and to place them in a conceptual framework that would be helpful to state and educational leaders in thinking about their options.

State governments, particularly higher education coordinating and governing boards, find themselves immersed in adult learning, not so much by choice as by virtue of the issues raised by the movement that require state-level attention. Issues are arising because of:

1. the proliferating number and variety of providers of adult learning services and the concomitant blurring of functions between those providers;
2. the increasing gap between those with little education and those who have more and want more still, raising concerns about which groups of adults states should concentrate their limited resources on;
3. the perceived need for new measures of quality assurance to assess the new kinds of programs designed to fit the unique learning needs of adults;

4. the shifting emphasis of job training programs from
   youth to adults, because adults will constitute the
   bulk of the workforce in need of new training to meet
   the changing needs of business and industry.

In some instances, governors and legislators have become directly involved in these issues, particularly in job
training initiatives, regulation of off-campus centers, and
tuition-waiver programs. But even in these cases, the state
higher education agency is usually assigned responsibility
for administering the program or enforcing the regulation.

How each state higher education agency approaches the
issues raised by the adult learning movement depends on
numerous factors: the philosophy of its leadership; the
statutory authority of the agency's board; the demographic
characteristics of the state's population; the history of
support for public higher education; the nature of the
state's industries and condition of its economy; and the
extent to which its colleges and universities are into the
business of serving adults. Such reliance on individual
state circumstances makes generalizations about appropriate state roles impossible. Nevertheless, what can be
gleaned from analysis of the information gathered in this
monograph is a better understanding of the options, placed
in the context of the concerns about lifelong learning.

The conceptual design for this analysis is three-tiered.
First, for any given issue, the state can take one of four
approaches: (1) It can take an essentially hands-off or laissez-
faire stance; (2) it can offer encouragement to adults to
learn and to providers to offer appropriate services; (3) it
can intervene to actively promote access or regulate quality; and (4) it can offer services or support directly.

Second, having arrived at an approach (either directly or
by default), methods must be chosen to implement it. The
methods from which the state agency can choose are typically those functions for which it has responsibility—for
example, planning, coordination, budget review, program
evaluation and approval, data collection, and development
of policy recommendations. Finally, these methods can be
further broken down into activities and policies that put
the approach into action. Policies provide a procedure for
making and implementing decisions about the area of con-

cern, whereas activities involve special programs or actions taken to address a particular situation.

So, for instance, if the *issue* is who should provide off-campus instruction, a state may choose to *approach* the problem through intervention. The *method* it chooses is regulation, adopting the *policy* that it will not support instruction offered more than 30 miles beyond a campus.

For each of the four approaches identified in this review of the literature is presented a justification for that approach, a list of the methods that have been used to implement it, and a review of some of the activities and policies that have emerged.

The Laissez-Faire Approach
Justification

Two reasons are apparent for the laissez-faire approach. First, a state may consciously choose a hands-off philosophy based on the belief that the state has no role in encouraging adult learning or interfering with college and university activities. Over time, the argument goes, adults will act in their own best interests and will seek the right kinds of learning services to meet their needs. In addition, the laissez-faire approach assumes that institutions will act responsibly in meeting those needs. In short, one justification for the laissez-faire approach lies in the belief that letting the free market prevail will best serve the interests of adults and providers.

Second, states may have no involvement in an adult education issue because nothing is happening to force them to take a position. This situation might occur when the state agency is unaware of a problem, lacks the statutory authority to do anything about it, cannot afford the staff time or resources to address it, or simply would rather not become involved.

Methods and activities/policies

The laissez-faire approach requires no implementing methods or activities; it is the absence of implementation that makes it laissez faire. Most laissez-faire approaches appear to be the result of no decision rather than a conscious decision not to get involved. Yet many states seem to have established limits regarding how far they will go in entering an issue. For example, with regard to *providers,* many states involve themselves in issues concerning relationships among formal educational institutions, but few are involved with relationships between higher education and business/industry, professional associations, unions, or community organizations. With regard to *access,* many states have worked to remove policies that discriminate against adults, but none have gone so far as to identify adults per se as an underrepresented class in need of equal opportunity programs. With regard to *quality,* states have involved themselves in program review but, with a few outstanding exceptions, have steered clear of taking positions on so-called nontraditional approaches to the granting of credit. With regard to *economic revitalization,* many states are initiating and funding job training programs, but they delegate provision of those services to colleges and schools.

All states have adopted the hands-off approach to at least some issues, and many states practice this stance with regard to all issues. Some states have done nothing or almost nothing about defining an appropriate state role in lifelong learning. Evidence for this assertion is found more in the absence of any mention of adult learning policies in state documents than in considered judgments about appropriate state roles. For the most part, the needs of adult learners have not yet been separated from the needs of traditional students and are therefore unlikely to appear in need of resolution.

Encouragement
Justification
States may decide that the best way to approach concerns about adult education is to encourage adults to learn and to encourage providers to respond. While the state takes no direct role, it supports the efforts of others to get involved. It is in the interest of the state to have a citizenry of lifelong learners, but the state can best promote that end by playing the role of facilitator and letting others provide direct service and support.

Method: Planning and setting goals
The most comprehensive planning and goal setting on adult education have been undertaken by the New York Re-

gents, whose goals for adult learning chart an ambitious course of comprehensive planning for the year 2000. Many other states have studied and made recommendations regarding various aspects of adult education. The planning documents seem to strive for a balance between enhancing opportunity for adults and maintaining standards of quality.

Method: Collecting and disseminating data

Many states have collected data and developed projections on adult education for a specific report. Most states have also assessed needs in some way. But few states identify important data elements that they wish to track on an ongoing basis.

One exception is Ohio's annual survey of noncredit continuing education offerings, which allows state officials to analyze the distinctive markets being carved out by Ohio's 115 postsecondary institutions. Another exception is New York's "Plan to Learn" campaign, which attempts to make adults aware of the importance of learning, the extent of present participation, and the variety, quality, and accessibility of learning opportunities in the state.

Method: Creating incentives

States are beginning to create inducements to encourage adults to learn and providers to offer services. Frequently, they are no cost or low cost to the states, but in other cases, the question is how funds are handled.

Massachusetts, for example, offers degree-granting authority to educational operations founded by businesses and corporations (under specified conditions). Providers now qualifying under these terms include a hospital, a manufacturer of computers, a consulting firm, and a banking institute.

Most states offer tuition-waiver programs for older adult learners, although one might dispute the extent to which these programs act as inducements to participate. States that fund fee waivers are providing an incentive to colleges to develop programs that will attract older learners, whereas those that do not count students whose fees are waived in FTE students are discouraging such initiative.

Some states have done nothing or almost nothing about defining an appropriate state role in lifelong learning.

Method: Promoting local cooperation

While many states may hope that local providers will cooperate, few have actively launched programs to encourage cooperative arrangements. Ohio, however, is one example of an all-out effort to promote cooperation between institutions of higher education and local businesses and industries. Promotional methods include workshops, a newsletter, brochures, task forces, and data gathering. The regional Work and Learning Councils established by the Board of Regents provide a structure for continuing exchange of information among educational institutions and the business community.

After considerable discussion, Vermont established the policy that planning for adult part-time learners should be done regionally and locally rather than statewide. To implement the policy, Vermont established regional councils and created a task force to promote regional cooperation.

Method: Establishing task forces

Many states have formed task forces to bring visibility and possibly resolution to issues of adult education. Often, recommendations from task forces appear later as sponsored legislation.

Iowa's Coordinating Committee on Continuing Education, for example, has task forces active throughout the year, with membership appropriate to the goal of each task force. Recent task forces have dealt with experiential learning, use of media in higher education, noncollegiate-sponsored instruction, and mandatory continuing education (Bing 1982, p. 16).

Utah's master planning task force for continuing education/community service has made recommendations to the Utah Telecommunications Authority and the state legislature promoting the increased use of distance learning technologies.

Method: Sponsoring conferences and seminars

As part of an effort to enhance adult learning services, eight education groups in Colorado with separate but related responsibilities for adult education came together for a two-day working conference in September 1981. The participants reviewed the findings of a statewide survey on important issues related to adult education and generated ideas for solving the challenges they presented.

Kansas held two "futures invention" workshops to develop goals for statewide adult education and to devise strategies for achieving those goals. One of the outcomes of the workshops was submission of a resolution to the Legislative Educational Planning Committee to serve as the basis for further legislative response to the goals.

Wisconsin's tradition of professional development opportunities for staff of its vocational/technical and adult education institutions includes a leadership seminar for new or potential supervisors, coordinators, and administrators.

Intervention
Justification
A higher education agency can justify intervention in adult education issues because, as a state-level body, it has an interest in promoting the most efficient and effective use of public resources and protecting its citizens against fraudulent or shoddy educational practices. Some issues will inevitably need resolution, and a state agency, more than any other party, can mediate a balance between statewide interests and individual justice. Resolving the issues may involve low-, medium-, or high-level intervention.

Method: Delegating responsibility for coordination
In this low-level form of intervention, the state seeks to avoid costly duplication among and competition between providers. A distinction is made between the promotion of local cooperation discussed under *encouragement* and the coordination discussed here under *intervention*. The latter results from a decision to intervene by requiring coordination and assigning responsibility for it, whereas in the former, the state simply establishes the conditions and creates the incentives to encourage cooperation.

Planning and coordination between providers must take place, but it is best done locally or regionally. The state establishes who or what the local planning mechanism will be. Kentucky, for example, makes its state universities responsible for extended-campus coordinating districts. California and Illinois let community college districts and neighboring school districts determine between themselves who will offer adult basic education, within certain parameters established by the state. And under a new Arizona law, providers of vocational education must coordinate their planning under the leadership of a community college district.

Method: Centralizing coordination
In this medium-level form of intervention, the state seeks to stave off disputes between providers before they happen by retaining responsibility for planning and coordination at the state level.

With the increased application of telecommunications technology for educational purposes, several states have established "watchdog" commissions to oversee this field. While other educational delivery issues may be amenable to local resolution, courses delivered by televised, audio, or computerized methods cross all local boundaries and become state-level (if not national) issues. Rhode Island's Higher Education Television Council was founded to coordinate the activities of all public and independent colleges, universities, and career schools as they develop telecourses for distribution through cable television companies. The Idaho legislature mandated centralized management of the state's three public television stations, which had previously been administered at the three host university campuses.

As a result, many states have settled on a mediated approach to resolving issues arising at off-campus centers. These states have found local resolution unworkable, but they also hesitate to establish rigid rules to govern all situations. Instead, the state establishes a process for approving off-campus and out-of-state programs and judges each case on its merits. In Virginia, for example, all out-of-state institutions must seek the approval of the State Council of Higher Education to operate in the commonwealth.

Method: Regulating providers
In this high-level form of intervention, the state establishes clear rules of the game and monitors institutional compliance with those rules. Because the state has broad authority over education, it can demand accountability from those who offer educational services. While the lines be-

tween them are not totally clear, some states' approach to resolving issues arising at off-campus centers goes beyond centralized coordination to full-scale intervention.

The comprehensive policy established by the Illinois Board of Higher Education probably crosses over the line. The policy sets forth goals, establishes criteria for approval, requires annual reports from providers, and allows for the board's periodic review. Texas took a less direct tack at regulating off-campus activity: The legislature simply reduced funding for those centers based on the amount of instruction taking place outside an institution's campus. The state also requires accreditation agencies to conduct separate evaluations of branch campus operations of independent institutions. Alabama has reduced off-campus offerings by 70 percent after the Commission on Higher Education was given statutory authority for review and approval.

As resources become scarce and institutions become more resourceful in finding ways to serve adults, states are increasingly penurious about what kinds of instruction are worthy of state support. Many states have established across-the-board policies about what is and is not eligible for state subsidy. Community college courses seem particularly subject to regulation, and most states now disallow any state support for courses of purely "avocational/recreational" purpose.

Direct Support and Services
Justification
In some instances, it may be more advantageous to offer an adult learning service statewide rather than locally. One state-level program may be less expensive than many local programs of similar nature; one state-level program also offers comparable service to adults no matter where they reside. Adult education opportunities should be expanded, but rather than have institutions reallocate existing monies to fund those services, the state can appropriate the money directly.

Method: Funding programs directly
This approach is the most direct one a state can take to launch job training programs. Community colleges have long been in the business of job training, but the time it

takes them to respond to a proposal is constrained by procedures for program approval. They lack necessary financial carrots to draw in the cooperation of business and industry, and they may have different ideas than state officials about what industries they should be training people for. Twenty-seven states have decided to enter more directly into job training programs in the hope that their citizenry can be better prepared to work in high-growth industries and to offer alternative skills to people who have been displaced from their previous jobs. Four states have chosen to appropriate funds directly to statewide distance delivery programs. They include the Indiana Higher Education Telecommunications System, Kentucky's Telecommunications Consortium, the LEARN/Alaska Network, and the University of Wisconsin–Extension's Instructional Communications System.

Method: Establishing statewide programs
New York's Program on Noncollegiate Sponsored Instruction began in 1974 as a pilot program to evaluate 102 courses taught by corporations. Today its catalog contains over 1,500 courses assessed as worthy of credit that can be used toward requirements for the New York Regents' External Degree Program.

Several statewide distance delivery programs have been developed through cooperative efforts of public institutions. For instance, the Kansas Regents sponsor a Continuing Education Network—TELENET—for the state's professionals needing continuing education credit.

The Statewide Testing and Assessment Center in New Jersey was established to facilitate the awarding of college credit for adult learning regardless of where or when that learning occurred.

When federal monies for educational information centers ran out, many states were forced to give up the business of providing information and guidance to adult learners. But Indiana has made its information service, the Training and Education Data Service, into a freestanding, not-for-profit corporation. The data service got its start from sponsorship by the governor's office and five state agencies. Similarly, the Regional Learning Service of New York, started with grants from foundations and federal agencies, has become an independent information and counseling agency serving adults throughout the state.

Summary

Although the purpose in conducting this study was not to determine the frequency or popularity of various state roles in addressing the new concerns arising in lifelong learning, some general impressions have been formed about preferred state roles.

Overall, *encouragement* is the most extensively used approach, particularly for improving access. *Direct support and services* is another approach to improving access for which several examples can be found. *Direct support* is also the basis for many efforts at economic revitalization. A number of states have chosen *intervention* to deal with issues of educational providers and quality assurance, generally in relation to activities at off-campus centers.

The activities chosen by the six states involved in the Lifelong Learning Project provide an interesting glimpse at how states see their role when given visibility and modest financial support to provide leadership in adult education. Each state was given wide leeway in choosing how to enhance adult learning services in their state, with the hope that "new models for collaborative planning" between providers of adult learning services would emerge (Cross and Hilton 1983). A summary of the project descriptions reveals that every activity engaged in by project states falls under the category of encouragement. Five of the six states conducted surveys, numerous conferences and workshops were convened, several task forces were established, and three states monitored or proposed relevant legislation. No state sought to increase its intervention or even to tackle the problems that lead to the need for intervention. When "enhancing adult learning" was determined to be the goal, these states saw their role as providing support services to help make it happen.

It seems likely, for the next decade at least, that this is where the potential for state leadership in adult education lies. All states could profit from having better information about who is providing learning services to adults and about what adult learning needs are and are not being met. Greater emphasis at the state level on planning for adult learning may offer institutions a clearer sense of direction about the state's commitment to these learners. Establishing local mechanisms today for resolving issues regarding providers may preclude the need for state intervention in those issues tomorrow. Convening state-level task forces to monitor developments in such fields as telecommunications technology offers a more cost-effective approach than letting each institution struggle to keep abreast. And as more, varied providers enter the picture, states may find themselves less and less able to regulate or coordinate services to adults. Instead, they may find their biggest contribution to be helping to publicize services available to meet the needs of adults and then helping adults find the best services for their needs.

APPENDIX A
NEW YORK STATE GOALS FOR
ADULT LEARNING SERVICES BY THE YEAR 2000

*The Goals are written in the present tense to emphasize that they
are to be considered from the perspective of the year 2000. Each
Goal is preceded by a needed change in direction.*

*The basic question in every case is: What must be done at the
State, regional, local, and institutional levels to be sure that the
Goal is achieved?*

Goal #1: The Public Interest in Adult Learning in 2000
Public policy assures that learning opportunities are available to
all adults regardless of age, sex, physical condition, racial and
ethnic background, economic and social status, intellectual ability, and learning style. Learning by adults is a natural continua-
tion and an integral part of all life experience. Anyone capable of
learning may acquire knowledge and/or skills at whatever pace is
appropriate in an environment compatible with individual need
and background.

This public policy is reflected in the allocation of public funds
for the education of adults and the provision of supporting community services. It assures that adults are actively involved in the
planning of learning services and have wide choice of services
that best meet their learning needs and styles at each stage of life.
Special efforts are made to develop educational opportunities that
attract and help those who experience difficulty in learning.

In the area of the core skills it is in the public interest that all
adults achieve minimum levels of competency. Opportunity to
achieve the core skills is, therefore, provided without charge.

The Board of Regents periodically defines what constitutes the
core skills and the standards and measures to be used in assessing their attainment. They make provisions for educational services needed to help attain the core skills and they determine
what is to be done to help individuals who cannot achieve minimum levels of competency in the core skills because of handicapping conditions but who want educational or employment opportunities.

In the area of vocational skills it is in the public interest that
business and industry have a pool of adequately trained and well
educated individuals to meet their needs and to make them better
able to compete effectively in national and world markets. To
create this pool, various forms of public funding are provided to
individuals in need of access to educational, training, retraining
and upgrading opportunities in fields in demand by business and
industry.

It is also in the public interest to assure that all persons have the opportunity to acquire competencies in the liberal arts and sciences. Arrangements for educational services and financial support assure that these opportunities are available regardless **of age, work or family responsibilities, or ability to pay.**

It is also in the public interest to assure that all persons have the opportunity to acquire competencies in the liberal arts and sciences. Arrangements for educational services and financial support assure that these opportunities are available regardless of age, work or family responsibilities, or ability to pay.

In addition to the diploma and degree programs usually associated with core, vocational, baccalaureate, and graduate studies, the vitality and quality of life in a State like New York require the availability of a wide array of less formal, usually noncredit, learning opportunities and the library and museum collections to support such learning. The most important public contribution to this availability is the support of such institutions as libraries, museums, public radio and television stations, and other educational and cultural resources. In addition, the public interest may justify support for specific opportunities.

Goal #2: Learning Communities in 2000
Communities actively encourage learning and use education to enrich the lives of all citizens and help solve community problems. Learning opportunities are provided at many locations to take into account the convenience of learners and the efficient use of all community facilities, including schools, colleges, libraries, museums, shopping centers, work sites, and other places where adults congregate. Many providers offer programs in a wide variety of locations and settings; for example, colleges offer programs in high schools, museums, shopping centers, and work places. There is increased sharing of sites; for example, a high school, a college, a BOCES, and a health service all offer programs at a public library or community center. Support services, such as childcare, counseling, and health and social services are also offered at many learning locations. Increased public transportation facilitates access in both urban and rural areas.

The home is an increasingly important learning site, and there is increased attention to the family as a learning unit. Through various media, including computers and television, information and instructional programs are available at home and work. Public policy encourages the use of media to support learning.

Goal #3: The Timing of Learning in 2000
Adults pursue learning continuously throughout life. The concept of lifelong learning is fully accepted. As a result, credentials,

when used, recognize accomplishments to date and not the end of learning. Scheduled learning activities take place at times governed by learners' needs through such arrangements as short-term offerings, modular learning packages, and flexible scheduling. Flexibility is the norm rather than the exception.

Learning is recognized as an integral part of most other life activities. For example, at work, employers provide educational opportunities. Such learning is regularly recognized in educational assessments. At times, periods of study alternate with periods of work. Use of technology further frees adults from time constraints in their pursuit of learning.

Goal #4: The Providers of Adult Learning in 2000
A competitive marketplace of educational providers sufficient to meet the needs of individuals and society is ensured through adequate financing of adult learning (see Goal 8) and minimum regulation consistent with quality assurance, consumer protection, and accountability for public funds (see Goal 6). Unnecessary duplication of services is minimized primarily through voluntary collaboration among educational and service providers in each community. Collaboration between educational providers, providers of other human services, and business and industry assures that quality services are provided at varied locations and at convenient times. Collaboration is encouraged by public incentives and the recognition of the mutual advantages that responsible collaboration brings.

All providers seek to develop the capacity of adults to direct their own learning and to share their learning with others.

In delivering services, providers employ qualified people, some of whom teach as a profession and have special competence to help adults learn and use all resources, including those made accessible through technology, and some of whom are employed because of competence in their own vocational area or other areas of specialization.

The Board of Regents determines which institutions are eligible for State and Federal funds to provide core skill instruction to persons beyond the age of compulsory school attendance who lack the core skills and choose not to attend their designated public school. Public and private institutions in each region may compete for eligibility, and one or more institutions, depending on community need, may be selected. Selection is based on a variety of factors, including the measured achievements of adults who have been previously served by an applicant. There are provisions governing funding of services to promote efficient achievement of intended outcomes. Funding is a shared Federal, State, and local school district responsibility (see Goal 8).

Students, in consultation with counselors, may choose among authorized providers.

Goal #5: Information and Guidance Services in 2000
Learner-oriented information and guidance services are available at convenient times to assist adults with personal, educational, job, and career planning. Services are well publicized. A State-supported network of education information centers provides certain basic services without charge. The centers and cooperating agencies:

a. Offer services to all individuals in each region at times and locations convenient to all segments of the community.
b. Maintain current information about available educational and support services, including social and job placement services.
c. Create public awareness of the availability of these services.
d. Make special efforts to reach and serve people who do not perceive the need for education as a way to cope with personal problems or who experience special difficulties in gaining access to learning opportunities.
e. Enable learners to make discriminating use of all forms of information about education, including the opinions of other learners about the programs in which they have participated (see Goal 6).
f. Serve as advocates for individuals in relationships with providers.

Goal #6: Quality Control in 2000
Informed choice by consumers and government regulation are complementary means for assuring quality of providers and their programs. Consumers with full information about programs and services are able to determine which programs and services continue to be offered (see Goal 5). The Board of Regents, the State Education Department, other governmental agencies, service providers, and voluntary associations share with adult learners responsibility for quality control as follows:

Adult learners:
1. Use the information available to make choices about their own learning requirements and the best means to achieve them.
2. In their decisions, examine alternative providers and programs, and weigh carefully the factors that differentiate among alternatives, including the relationship between price and quality.

3. Inform appropriate voluntary and governmental agencies of provider violations of standards or prescribed procedures.

The Board of Regents and the
State Education Department:
1. Determine categories of providers subject to regulation, including providers offering substantial programs and those that use public funds or offer credentials recognized by the State.
2. Set minimum standards for achieving acceptable levels of quality and determine which providers meet those standards. Providers that do not meet the minimum standards are not eligible to receive public funds and may be prohibited from operating.
3. Set standards for information to be supplied by all providers and enforce those standards.
4. Obtain data on achievement of institutional objectives and on assessment of provider services, including those of voluntary accrediting associations.
5. Establish procedure for systematically obtaining the opinions of learners regarding the courses and programs in which they have participated and make that information available in an appropriate manner to the respective providers and other learners.
6. In cooperation with other governmental agencies, protect consumers against misrepresentation and similar abuses.

Providers:
1. Establish and publish procedures for assuring the quality of their services.
2. Provide prospective students with full information on all matters affecting their educational programs, including financial arrangements.
3. Maintain staffs qualified to perform in accordance with their own stated goals and policies.

Voluntary accrediting and other
associations:
1. Assist providers to maintain and improve quality.
2. Inform the public concerning the standards they apply in judging quality.
3. Assist the Education Department and other public agencies in identifying providers that fail to meet the standards of quality.

Goal #7: Assessment of Learning Outcomes in 2000
Individuals may seek assessment of the results of their learning efforts from specialized assessment agencies at any stage of their educational development. They may use the results to develop their educational and career plans and may make them available to employers when seeking employment or promotion. The agencies use many assessment procedures, not only paper and pencil tests, to determine the kind and level of competencies achieved. The competencies to be measured are developed with the involvement of employers, educators, government, and the public, and may be acquired through formal or informal learning or through life experience. Learners may have assessment results recorded in a national credit bank.

Comparable study undertaken anywhere is given comparable recognition by both educational providers and others who use the results of the assessment. For example, degree-granting institutions give credit for comparable work resulting from instruction sponsored by business, labor, the military, schools, or community organizations. Credit is always given only for competencies achieved, not for experience or participation in a course or other activity.

Goal #8: Financing Adult Learning in 2000
The economic, societal, and personal benefits of lifelong learning opportunities are recognized in public policy. Public financing of adult learning is an expansion of the traditional commitment to public support of education for children and youth. It is based on the recognition that there are social benefits in meeting certain adult learning needs. These benefits include assurance that most adults attain competency in the core skills, that there is a trained work force to meet the needs of the State's economy, and that individuals have the education to develop as full human beings and have the capacity to cope with an increasingly complex world.

As a foundation for all forms of adult learning from independent study to formal courses in schools and colleges, the State provides funding to a broad array of institutions and services, including schools, BOCES, colleges, universities, libraries and library systems, museums, radio and television services, information and counseling centers, and artistic organizations (see Goal 6 for provisions determining eligibility). Funding levels ensure high quality services to residents in all parts of the State. Such institutional aid is used primarily to build the capacity of institutions to deliver services, promote collaboration, and ensure the availability of essential services.

However, because of the public interest in assuring that all adults attain competency in the core skills, certain institutions receive public funds to provide education in these skills free of charge to adults lacking such skills. The Board of Regents determines the standards for core skill competency and the conditions under which funding will be provided (see Goal 4).

For educational levels beyond the core, adults are generally expected to pay for the services they require either from personal resources or with help from their employers. However, educational funds for which youth are eligible are available to adults on an equitable basis. In addition, because some essential individual and societal learning needs may not be met through private efforts alone, public funds are used to supplement private resources. Such aid is usually provided on the basis of need and is given in a manner that maximizes the freedom of the adult to choose the time, place and circumstances of learning.

Conclusion

If the eight Goals are realized, we may find the following changes in our society:

- Learning by adults is recognized, encouraged, and supported as a matter of public policy.
- Learning occurs throughout the community at places and times convenient to adult learners.
- Providers of services collaborate to assure a full range of offerings and effective use of resources.
- New learning technologies are widely used at home and at work.
- All who need instruction in the core skills receive it free of charge.
- Information and guidance services are readily available.
- Informed consumer choice assures high quality services from all providers.
- Appropriate recognition for learning is provided, so that however achieved, educational accomplishment can be validated and used for occupational advancement, entry to advanced study, or other purposes.
- Adult learners and the private sector provide most of the support for learning opportunities.
- Public funding plays a key role in assuring the availability of learning services and access to them.

REFERENCES

The ERIC Clearinghouse on Higher Education abstracts and indexes the current literature on higher education for the National Institute of Education's monthly bibliographic journal *Resources in Education*. Most of these publications are available through the ERIC Document Reproduction Service (EDRS). For publications cited in this list that are available from EDRS, ordering number and price are included. Readers who wish to order a publication should write to the ERIC Document Reproduction Service, P.O. Box 190, Arlington, Virginia 22210. When ordering, please specify the document number. Documents are available as noted in microfiche (MF) and paper copy (PC). As prices are subject to change, it is advisable to check the latest issue of *Resources in Education* for current cost based on the number of pages in the publication.

Aaron, Henry J. 1978. *Politics and the Professors: The Great Society in Perspective*. Washington, D.C.: The Brookings Institution.

Anderson, R. E., and Darkenwald, G. G. 1979. *Participation and Persistence in American Adult Education*. New York: The College Board. ED 181 186. 58 pp. MF–$1.17; PC not available EDRS.

Andrews, Grover. 1978. *Assessing Nontraditional Education: A Summary of the Project Report*. Washington, D.C.: Commission on Postsecondary Accreditation. ED 165 577. 222 pp. MF–$1.17; PC–$18.53.

Astin, Alexander. 1977. *Four Critical Years*. San Francisco: Jossey-Bass.

———. 1982. *Minorities in American Higher Education*. San Francisco: Jossey-Bass.

Bailey, Stephen. 1979. *Academic Quality Control: The Case of College Programs on Military Bases*. Washington, D.C.: American Association of Higher Education. ED 213 271. 64 pp. MF–$1.17; PC not available EDRS.

Becker, Gary S. 1975. *Human Capital*. 2d ed. New York: National Bureau of Economic Research.

Bing, Linda West. 1982. *State Policies and Programs in Support of Adult Learning: A Survey of Selected States*. Denver: Education Commission of the States. ED 235 389. 85 pp. MF–$1.17; PC–$9.37.

Bluestone, Barry. 1968. "Lower-Income Workers and Marginal Industries." In *Poverty in America*, edited by Louis Ferman et al. Ann Arbor: The University of Michigan Press.

Botkin, James; Dimancescu, Dan; and Stata, Ray. 1982. *Global*

Stakes: The Future of High Technology in America. Cambridge, Mass.: Ballinger Publishing Co.

Bowen, Frank; Edelstein, Stewart; and Medsker, Leland. 1979. "The Identification of Decisionmakers Concerned with Nontraditional Degree Programs and an Analysis of Their Information Needs." In *An Evaluative Look at Nontraditional Postsecondary Education,* edited by Charles Stalford. Washington, D.C.: National Institute of Education. ED 176 106. 194 pp. MF–$1.17; PC–$16.76.

Bowen, Howard R.; Ulcak, Jacqueline; Dodd, Powers; and Douglass, Gordon K. 1977. *Investment in Learning: The Individual and Social Value of American Higher Education.* San Francisco: Jossey-Bass.

Breneman, David W., and Nelson, Susan C. 1981. *Financing Community Colleges: An Economic Perspective.* Washington, D.C.: The Brookings Institution.

Brown, Albert W. 1982. "Voluntary Education Programs for Military Personnel." Mimeographed.

California Community Colleges. 1982. "Fee Contingency Plan." Sacramento: Board of Governors.

California Higher Education. July 1983. "Learn for Fee" 1: 14–15.

Capon, Noel. 1981. *Note on the Product Life Cycle.* Boston: Harvard Business School.

– Carp, A.; Peterson, R.; and Roelfs, P. 1974. "Adult Learning Interests and Experiences." In *Planning Non-Traditional Programs,* edited by K. P. Cross, J. R. Valley, and Associates. San Francisco: Jossey-Bass.

Champanis, A. 1971. "Prelude to 2001: Exploration in Communications." *American Psychologist* 26: 949–61.

Chickering, Arthur. 1974. *Commuting versus Resident Students.* San Francisco: Jossey-Bass.

Choate, Pat. 1983. "American Workers at the Rubicon: A National Human Resource Strategy." Washington, D.C.: Business–Higher Education Forum.

Cohen, Arthur M., and Brawer, Florence B. 1982. *The American Community College.* San Francisco: Jossey-Bass.

Coordinating Board, Texas College and University System. 1974. *Thrust for Relevance.* Report of the Statewide Study on Adult and Continuing Education. Austin: Coordinating Board.

Council on Postsecondary Accreditation. 1983a. *Policy Statement on Off-Campus Credit Programs.* Washington, D.C.: COPA.

———. 1983b. *Postsecondary Educational Programs on Military Bases.* Washington, D.C.: COPA.

Craig, R. L., and Evers, C. J. 1981. "Employers as Educators: The 'Shadow Educational System.' " In *Business and Higher Education: Toward New Alliances,* edited by Gerald Gold. New Directions for Experiential Learning No. 13. San Francisco: Jossey-Bass.

Craven, Eugene C. 1980. *Academic Program Evaluation.* New Directions for Institutional Research No. 27. San Francisco: Jossey-Bass.

Cross, K. Patricia. 1978. *The Missing Link: Connecting Adult Learners to Learning Resources.* New York: The College Board. ED 163 177. 87 pp. MF–$1.17; PC not available EDRS.

———. 1981. *Adults as Learners.* San Francisco: Jossey-Bass.

———. 1983. "The State of the Art in Needs Assessments." *Community/Junior College Quarterly* 7: 195–206.

Cross, K. Patricia, and Hilton, William J. 1983. *Enhancing the State Role in Lifelong Learning: A Summary Report of a Project.* Denver: Education Commission of the States. ED 235 390. 62 pp. MF–$1.17; PC–$7.24.

Cross, K. P., and Zusman, Ami. 1979. "The Needs of Nontraditional Learners and the Responses of Nontraditional Programs." In *An Evaluative Look at Nontraditional Postsecondary Education,* edited by Charles Stalford. Washington, D.C.: National Institute of Education.

"Customized Training." December/January 1982–83. *Community and Junior College Journal* 53: 10–11.

Davis, Ronnie J., and Morrall, John F., II. 1974. *Evaluating Educational Investment.* Lexington, Mass.: Lexington Books.

Dinkelspiel, J. R. 1981. "Education and Training Programs at Xerox." In *Workplace Perspectives on Education and Training,* edited by P. B. Doeringer. Boston: Kluwer-Nijhoff.

Doeringer, Peter, and Piore, Michael. 1971. *Internal Labor Markets and Manpower Analysis.* Lexington, Mass.: D.C. Heath & Co.

Edgerton, Russell. June 1983. "A College Education up to Beating the Japanese." *American Association for Higher Education Bulletin* 35: 3–7 + .

Education Commission of the States. 1977. *Final Report and Recommendation: Task Force on State, Institutional, and Federal Responsibilities in Providing Post-Secondary Educational Opportunities to Service Personnel.* Denver: Education Commission of the States.

———. 1981. *Higher Education in the States* 7(8). Denver: Education Commission of the States.

———. 1982. *Higher Education in the States* 8(2). Denver: Education Commission of the States.

Edwards, Richard G.; Reich, Michael; and Gordon, David, eds. 1975. *Labor Market Segmentation*. Lexington, Mass.: D.C. Heath & Co.

Feldstein, Martin. Fall 1973. "The Economics of the New Unemployment." *The Public Interest* (33): 3–42.

Floyd, Carol Everly. 1982. *State Planning, Budgeting, and Accountability: Approaches for Higher Education*. AAHE-ERIC/Higher Education Research Report No. 7. Washington, D.C.: American Association for Higher Education. ED 224 452. 58 pp. MF–$1.17; PC–$7.24.

Folger, John, ed. 1977. *Increasing the Public Accountability of Higher Education*. New Directions for Institutional Research No. 16. San Francisco: Jossey-Bass.

Freeman, Richard. 1976. *The Declining Economic Value of Higher Education and the American Society*. An Occasional Paper of the Aspen Institute for Humanistic Studies. New York: Aspen Institute Program on Education for a Changing Society. ED 146 877. 37 pp. MF–$1.17; PC–$5.49.

Garrison, Don C. 1980. "Community Colleges and Industry: A Stronger Partnership for Human Resource Development." In *Employee Training for Productivity*, edited by Rober Yarrington. Washington, D.C.: American Association for Community and Junior Colleges. ED 190 188. 30 pp. MF–$1.17; PC not available EDRS.

George Meany Center for Labor Studies. 1983–84. *1983–84 Catalog*. Silver Spring, Md.: Meany Center for Labor Studies.

Gleazer, Edmund J., Jr. 1980. *The Community College: Values, Vision, and Vitality*. Washington, D.C.: American Association for Community and Junior Colleges. ED 187 364. 197 pp. MF–$1.17; PC not available EDRS.

Gold, G. G. 1981. "Toward Business–Higher Education Alliances." In *Business and Higher Education: Toward New Alliances*, edited by G. G. Gold. New Directions for Experiential Learning No. 13. San Francisco: Jossey-Bass.

Goldstein, Harold. 1980. *Worker Education and Training Policies Project*. Washington, D.C.: National Institute for Work and Learning.

Goldstein, Michael. 1981. "A Survey of Key Policy Issues Affecting Higher Education and the Adult Learner." Photocopy. Discussion draft for use by the ACE Commission on Higher Education and the Adult Learner.

Harrison, Bennett. Spring 1972. "Employment, Unemployment, and Structure of the Urban Labor Market." *The Wharton Quarterly* 6:4–7 + .

Hilton, William J. 1983. *Reaching out to Adult Learners: The*

Why and the How of Lifelong Learning. Denver: Education Commission of the States/Kellogg Foundation Lifelong Learning Project.

Howard, Robert. September/October 1981. "Second Class in Silicon Valley." *Working Papers Magazine* 8:20–31.

Hunter, Carman St. John, and Harmon, David. 1979. *Adult Illiteracy in the United States: A Report to the Ford Foundation*. New York: McGraw-Hill.

IBM Systems Research Institute. 1981. *Bulletin*. New York: IBM Systems Research Institute.

Illinois Board of Higher Education. 1983. *Board of Higher Education Policies Related to the Review and Approval of Off-Campus Programs of Public Universities, Independent Colleges and Universities, and Out-of-State Institutions*. Springfield: Illinois Board of Higher Education.

Indiana Commission for Higher Education. 1983. *Annual Report: 1982*. Indianapolis: Indiana Commission for Higher Education.

Jacobs, Frederic, and Allen, Richard J., eds. 1982. *Expanding the Missions of Graduate and Professional Education*. New Directions for Experiential Learning No. 15 . San Francisco: Jossey-Bass.

Jonsen, Richard W. May 1978. "Lifelong Learning: State Policies." *School Review* 86:360–81.

Keeton, Morris T., ed. 1980. *Defining and Assuring Quality in Experiential Learning*. New Directions for Experiential Learning No. 9. San Francisco: Jossey-Bass.

Kirkwood, Robert. 1981. "Process or Outcomes: A False Dichotomy." In *Quality: Higher Education's Principal Challenge*, edited by T.M. Stauffer. Washington, D.C.: American Council on Education.

Knapp, Joan E., ed. 1981. *Financing and Implementing Prior Learning Assessment*. New Directions for Experiential Learning No. 14. San Francisco: Jossey-Bass.

Knapp, Joan E., and Jacobs, Paul I. 1981. *Setting Standards for Assessing Experiential Learning*. Columbia, Md.: Council for the Advancement of Experiential Learning. ED 212 665. 32 pp. MF–$1.17; PC not available EDRS.

Kurland, Norman. 1983. "The New York State Case." In *Enhancing the State Role in Lifelong Learning: Case Studies of Six Pilot States*. Denver: Education Commission of the States. ED 235 343. 79 pp. MF–$1.17; PC–$9.37.

Kurland, Norman D.; Purga, Robert L.; and Hilton, William J. 1982. *Financing Adult Learning: Spotlight on the States*. Denver: Education Commission of the States/Lifelong Learning Project. ED 235 387. 63 pp. MF–$1.17; PC–$7.24.

Kuttner, Bob. July 1983. "The Declining Middle." *The Atlantic Monthly* 252:60–72.

Levin, Henry M. May 1978. "Financing Higher Education and Social Equity: Implications for Lifelong Learning." *School Review* 86: 327–47.

Levin, Henry M., and Rumberger, Russell N. 1983. *The Educational Implications of High Technology.* Palo Alto, Calif.: Institute for Research on Educational Finance and Governance, Stanford University School of Education. ED 229 879. 24 pp. MF–$1.17; PC–$3.74.

Lewis, Raymond. 1983. *Meeting Learners' Needs through Telecommunications: A Directory and Guide to Programs.* Washington, D.C.: American Association for Higher Education. ED 227 731. 260 pp. MF–$1.17; PC not available EDRS.

Long, H. B. 1980. "Characteristics of Senior Citizens' Educational Tuition Waivers in 21 States: A Followup Study." *Educational Gerontology* 5: 139–99.

Lublin, Joan. 29 July 1983. How to Help Displaced Workers?" *Wall Street Journal.*

Lusterman, Seymour. 1977. *Education in Industry.* New York: The Conference Board.

Lynton, Ernest A. Fall 1982. "Improving Cooperation between Colleges and Corporations." *Educational Record* 63: 20–23.

McClure, Shirley. 1983. *State Strategic Planning for Technology.* ECS Issuegram #38. Denver: Education Commission of the States. ED 234 737. 8 pp. MF–$1.17; PC–$3.74.

McGarraghy, John J., and Reilly, Kevin P. 1981. "College Credit for Corporate Training." In *Business and Higher Education: Toward New Alliances,* edited by Gerald G. Gold. New Directions for Experiential Learning No. 13. San Francisco: Jossey-Bass.

Mackin, Christopher. 1983. *Strategies for Local Ownership and Control: A Policy Analysis.* Somerville, Mass.: Industrial Cooperative Association.

McPherson, Michael. 1982. "Higher Education: Investment or Expense." In *Financing Higher Education: The Public Investment,* edited by John G. Hoy and Melvin H. Bernstein. Boston: Auburn House Publishing Co.

MacTaggart, Terrence, ed. 1983. *Cost Effective Assessment of Prior Learning.* New Directions for Experiential Learning No. 19. San Francisco: Jossey-Bass.

Magarrell, Jack. 23 February 1983a. "Governors See Higher Education as Key to Economic Recovery." *Chronicle of Higher Education.*

————. 9 March 1983b. "Governors Warned about Weaknesses

of Colleges in High-Technology Areas." *Chronicle of Higher Education.*

Marcus, L. R.; Leone, A. O.; and Goldberg, E. D. 1983. *The Path to Excellence: Quality Assurance in Higher Education.* **ASHE-ERIC Higher Education Research Report No. 1.** Washington, D.C.: Association for the Study of Higher Education. ED 235 697. 83 pp. MF–$1.17; PC–$9.37.

Martorana, S. V., and Kuhns, Eileen. 1983. *A Report to the Fund for the Improvement of Postsecondary Education (FIPSE) on the Project "Cooperative Regional Planning and Action to Enhance Postsecondary Education across State Lines."* University Park, Pa.: The Pennsylvania State University and Catholic University of America.

Maryland State Board for Community Colleges. 1978. *Continuing Education Manual.* Annapolis: Maryland State Board for Community Colleges. ED 154 899. 29 pp. MF–$1.17; PC–$5.49.

Massachusetts Institute of Technology. 1982. *Lifelong Cooperative Education.* Cambridge, Mass.: MIT, Department of Electrical Engineering and Computer Science.

Medoff, James L. 1982. "Formal Training and Labor Productivity." In *The Nature and Extent of Employee Training and Development.* A State-of-the-Art Forum on Data Gathering. Washington, D.C.: American Society for Training and Development.

Metty, Michael. Spring 1983. "Looking Backward, Forward, and Inward: Some Policy Considerations for Telecommunications." *University of Alaska Magazine* 1: 27–29.

Millard, Richard. 1983. "A Council on Postsecondary Accreditation View of Education in the Military." Speech delivered in Bad Kissingen, Germany, 3 March.

Minnesota Higher Education Coordinating Board. 1981. *Post-Secondary Education for Part-Time and Returning Students.* Minneapolis: Minnesota Higher Education Coordinating Board.

Moore, Ann H.; Settle, Theodore J.; and Skinner, Patricia A. 1983. "Strengthening College/Company Cooperation: An Ohio Perspective." Photocopy. Paper presented to the National University Continuing Education Association, 10–13 October, Las Vegas, Nevada. ED 230 078. 14 pp. MF–$1.17; PC–$3.74.

National Center for Education Statistics. 1981. "Women and Minority Groups Make Up Largest Segment of Adult Basic and Secondary Education Programs." *NCES Bulletin.*

———. 1982. *Participation in Adult Education: 1981.* Washington, D.C.: National Center for Education Statistics. ED 221 751. 43 pp. MF–$1.17; PC–$5.49.

————. 1983. *The Condition of Education: 1983*. Washington, D.C.: National Center for Education Statistics. ED 233 476. 283 pp. MF–$1.17; PC–$24.14.

National Governors Association and the National Association of State Budget Officers. 1983. *Fiscal Survey of the States: 1983*. Washington, D.C.: National Governors Association and the National Association of State Budget Officers.

National Science Foundation. 1980. *Science and Engineering Education for the 1980s and Beyond*. Washington, D.C.: National Science Foundation. ED 193 092. 228 pp. MF–$1.17; PC–$20.64.

Nebraska Coordinating Commission for Postsecondary Education. 1978. *1978 Goals and Recommendations for Adult and Continuing Education Instructional Programs of Nebraska Postsecondary Institutions*. Lincoln: Nebraska Coordinating Commission for Postsecondary Education. ED 163 161. 59 pp. MF–$1.17; PC–$7.24.

New York State Education Department. 1981. "New York State Goals for Adult Learning Services by the Year 2000." Albany: Office of Adult Learning Services, State Education Department, University of the State of New York. ED 215 231. 20 pp. MF–$1.17; PC–$3.74.

————. 1981–82a. *Inside Education*. Annual Report: 1981–82, vol. 69, no. 2. Albany: New York State Education Department.

————. 1981–82b. "Student Aid and the Financing of Higher Education." Photocopy. A discussion paper for use at the 1981–82 Regents/Commissioners Regional Conferences. Albany: The University of the State of New York. ED 212 238. 27 pp. MF–$1.17; PC–$5.49.

————. 1982. *"Plan to Learn": A Public Awareness Program for Adult Learning in New York State*. Albany: Office of Adult Learning Services, State Education Department.

Nolfi, George. 1982. "Issues in Lifelong Learning: Investing in Human Capital." Photocopy. Paper prepared for the Education Commission of the States/Lifelong Learning Project.

Office of Technology Assessment, Congress of the United States. 1982. *Informational Technology and Its Impact on American Education*. Washington, D.C.: U.S. Government Printing Office.

Ohio Board of Regents. 1982a. *Employer-Sponsored Instruction: Focus on Ohio Business and Industry*. Columbus: Ohio Board of Regents. ED 218 459. 64 pp. MF–$1.17; PC–$7.24.

————. 1982b. *Master Plan for Higher Education: Opportunity in a Time of Change*. Columbus: Ohio Board of Regents. ED 227 742. 48 pp. MF–$1.17; PC–$5.49.

————. 1982c. *Ohio Resource Network: Mobilizing Colleges and Universities to Benefit Business and Industry.* Columbus: Ohio Board of Regents.

————. 1982d. *A Report on Non-Credit Continuing Education Activities in Ohio: 1980–81.* Columbus: Ohio Board of Regents.

Oregon Educational Coordinating Commission. 1976. *Adult/ Continuing Education in Oregon.* Salem: Oregon Educational Coordinating Commission.

————. 1980. *Access to Postsecondary Educational Services; Part 2: Off-Campus Instruction.* Salem: Oregon Educational Coordinating Commission.

Parnell, Dale. December/January 1982–83. "Labor/Industry/ College Partnership Breaks New Ground." *Community and Junior College Journal* 53: 16–20.

————. March 1983. "Governor Calls for National Employment Policy with Role for Community Colleges." *Community and Junior College Journal* 53: 14–17.

Petersen, Dorothy G. 1981. "Quality of Accreditation: To Measure by Process or Outcomes?" In *Quality: Higher Education's Principal Challenge,* edited by T. M. Stauffer. Washington, D.C.: American Council on Education.

Peterson, R. E., and Associates. 1979. *Lifelong Learning in America.* San Francisco: Jossey-Bass.

Peterson, R. E., and Hefferlin, J. B. 1975. *Postsecondary Alternatives to Meet the Educational Needs of California's Adults.* Sacramento: Postsecondary Alternatives Study.

Pickens, William H. 1980. "Hard Times for Recurrent Education? Predictions for California during the 1980s." Paper presented to a seminar on the Cost of Financing Recurrent Education, 11 July, Palo Alto. ED 206 341. 12 pp. MF–$1.17; PC–$3.74.

Piore, Michael. 1970. "Jobs and Training." In *The State and the Poor,* edited by Beer and Barringer. Boston: Winthrop Publishers.

Polaroid Corporation. 1981. *Fall 1981 Courses.* Cambridge, Mass.: Human Resource Development Group.

Pollack, Andrew. 27 February 1983. "The Birth of Silicon Statesmanship." *The New York Times.*

Porat, Marc Uri. 1977. *The Information Economy.* 9 vols. Washington, D.C.: U.S. Government Printing Office.

Program on Noncollegiate Sponsored Instruction. 1982. *A Guide to Educational Programs in Noncollegiate Organizations.* Albany: University of the State of New York. ED 219 550. 460 pp. MF–$1.17; PC–$37.55.

Purdy, Leslie N. 1980. "The History of Television and Radio in

Continuing Education." In *Providing Continuing Education by Media and Technology,* edited by Martin N. Chamberlain. New Directions for Continuing Education No. 5. San Francisco: Jossey-Bass.

Rehnke, Mary Ann F., ed. 1982–83. *Liberal Learning and Career Preparation.* Current Issues in Higher Education No. 2. Washington, D.C.: American Association for Higher Education.

Reich, Michael; Gordon, David M.; and Edwards, Richard C. May 1973. "A Theory of Labor Market Segmentation." *American Economic Review* 63. Reprinted in *Problems in Political Economy: An Urban Perspective,* edited by David M. Gordon. Lexington, Mass.: D.C. Heath & Co., 1977.

Richardson, Penelope. 1980. "Adapting 'Distance Learning' Instruction to Adult Differences." Photocopy. Los Angeles: University of Southern California. ED 210 498. 28 pp. MF–$1.17; PC–$5.49.

Romaniuk, Jean Gasen. 1982. *The Older Adult in Higher Education: An Analysis of State Public Policy.* Washington, D.C.: National Council on the Aging.

Schultz, Theodore W. September 1975. "The Value of the Ability to Deal with Disequilibria." *Journal of Economic Literature* 13: 827–46.

Shipton, Jane, and Steltenpohl, Elizabeth. 1981. "Relating Assessment of Prior Learning to Educational Planning." New Directions for Experiential Learning No. 14. San Francisco: Jossey-Bass.

Simosko, Susan. 1983. *Final Report to the Fund for the Improvement of Postsecondary Education (FIPSE) on the Establishment of the Statewide Testing and Assessment Center.* Trenton, N.J.: Edison State College.

Skinner, Patricia A., and Moore, Ann H. 1983. "The Ohio Case." In *Enhancing the State Role in Lifelong Learning: Case Studies of the Six Pilot States.* Denver: Education Commission of the States. ED 235 343. 79 pp. MF–$1.17; PC–$10.37.

Sosdian, C.P. 1978. *External Degrees: Program and Student Characteristics.* Washington, D.C.: National Institute of Education. ED 152 174. 65 pp. MF–$1.17; PC–$7.24.

South Carolina State Board for Technical and Comprehensive Education. n.d. *Planning for Profit, Progress, and Productivity.* Columbia, S.C.: State Board for Technical and Comprehensive Education.

Stadtman, Verne A. 1980. *Academic Adaptations: Higher Education Prepares for the 1980s and 1990s.* San Francisco: Jossey-Bass.

Stauffer, T. M., ed. 1981. *Quality: Higher Education's Principal*

Challenge. Washington, D.C.: American Council on Education.

Steinbacher, Roberta. 14 April 1983. Memo to Edward Q. Moulton, Chancellor of the Ohio Board of Regents.

Stern, Milton. 1979. "Competition in Continuing Education in the 80s." Unpublished paper delivered at the Annual Conference of the Universities Council for Adult Education, 11 April, University of Keele, U.K.

————. 1983. "How Can We Keep Them Educated?" Speech delivered at the 1983 Colloquium Series, Division of Higher and Adult Continuing Education, University of Michigan, 22 March, Ann Arbor, Michigan.

Stringer, Herbert. 1980. "The Joint Role of Industry and Education in Human Resource Development." Photocopy. Wingspread Conference on Industry-Education Cooperation sponsored by the American Vocational Association, the American Society for Training and Development, and the American Association of Community and Junior Colleges, 12–14 March.

Tri-County Technical College. 1982. *1981–82 Annual Report to the People.* Pendleton, S.C.: Tri-County Technical College.

Tucker, Marc S. 1982. "The Turning Point: Telecommunications and Higher Education in the 1980s." Photocopy. Washington, D.C.: Project on Information Technology and Education.

U.S. Bureau of the Census. 1977. "Educational Attainment in the United States: March 1977 and 1976." *Current Population Reports,* Series P-20, no. 314. Washington, D.C.: U.S. Government Printing Office.

————. 1982. "Population Profile of the United States: 1981." *Current Population Reports,* Series P-20, no. 374. Washington, D.C.: U.S. Government Printing Office.

U.S. Department of Health, Education, and Welfare. 1978. *Lifelong Learning and Public Policy.* Washington, D.C.: Lifelong Learning Project.

Useem, Elizabeth. 1982. "Education in a High-Technology World: The Case of Route 128." Photocopy. Boston: Institute for the Interdisciplinary Study of Education, Northeastern University. ED 222 108. 83 pp. MF–$1.17; PC–$9.37.

Wallhaus, Robert, and Rock, Timothy. 1983. "The Illinois Case." In *Enhancing the State Role in Lifelong Learning.* Denver: Education Commission of the States. ED 235 343. 79 pp. MF–$1.17; PC–$9.37.

Warren, Russell. 1983. *New Links between General Education and Business Careers.* Washington, D.C.: American Association of Colleges. ED 230 117. 35 pp. MF–$1.17; PC not available EDRS.

Watcke, Ronald R. December/January 1982–83. "Partnership Vital to High Tech." *Community and Junior College Journal* 53: 28–31 + .

Weinstein, L. M. 1982. "Labor Unions." In *The Costs and Financing of Adult Education and Training,* edited by R. E. Anderson and E. S. Kasl. Lexington, Mass.: Lexington Books.

Welch, Finis. January/February 1970. "Education in Production." *Journal of Political Economy* 78: 35–59.

Wells, Louis J., Jr., ed. 1972. *The Product Life Cycle and International Trade.* Boston: Harvard Business School.

White House Conference on Aging. 1971. *Toward a National Policy on Aging: Final Report.* Vol. 2. Washington, D.C.: U.S. Government Printing Office.

Whitelaw, W., ed. 1982–83. "The Economy and the College Student." In *Liberal Learning and Career Preparation,* edited by Mary Ann F. Rehnke. Current Issues in Higher Education No. 2. Washington, D.C.: American Association for Higher Education.

Young, Robert B. 1981. "The Evaluation of Community Education in Community and Junior Colleges." In *A Look to Future Years: Prospects Regarding the Scope and Process of Community Organization,* edited by Holly M. Jellison. Monograph No. 4. Center for Community Education. Washington, D.C.: American Association for Community and Junior Colleges. ED 206 365. 69 pp. MF–$1.17; PC not available EDRS.

ASHE-ERIC HIGHER EDUCATION RESEARCH REPORTS

Starting in 1983, the Association for the Study of Higher Education assumed cosponsorship of the Higher Education Research Reports with the ERIC Clearinghouse on Higher Education. For the previous 11 years, ERIC and the American Association for Higher Education prepared and published the reports.

Each report is the definitive analysis of a tough higher education problem, based on a thorough research of pertinent literature and institutional experiences. Report topics, identified by a national survey, are written by noted practitioners and scholars with prepublication manuscript reviews by experts.

Ten monographs in the ASHE-ERIC Higher Education Research Report series are published each year, available individually or by subscription. Subscription to 10 issues is $55 regular; $40 for members of AERA, AAHE, and AIR; $35 for members of ASHE. (Add $7.50 outside U.S.)

Prices for single copies, including 4th class postage and handling, are $7.50 regular and $6.00 for members of AERA, AAHE, AIR, and ASHE. If faster first-class postage is desired for U.S. and Canadian orders, for each publication ordered add $.75; for overseas, add $4.50. For VISA and MasterCard payments, give card number, expiration date, and signature. Orders under $25 must be prepaid. Bulk discounts are available on orders of 10 or more of a single title. Order from the Publications Department, Association for the Study of Higher Education, One Dupont Circle, Suite 630, Washington, D.C. 20036, (202) 296-2597. Write for a complete list of Higher Education Research Reports and other ASHE and ERIC publications.

1981 Higher Education Research Reports

1. Minority Access to Higher Education
   Jean L. Preer

2. Institutional Advancement Strategies in Hard Times
   Michael D. Richards and Gerald Sherratt

3. Functional Literacy in the College Setting
   Richard C. Richardson, Jr., Kathryn J. Martens, and Elizabeth C. Fisk

4. Indices of Quality in the Undergraduate Experience
   George D. Kuh

5. Marketing in Higher Education
   Stanley M. Grabowski

6. Computer Literacy in Higher Education
   Francis E. Masat

7. Financial Analysis for Academic Units
   Donald L. Walters

8. Assessing the Impact of Faculty Collective Bargaining
   J. Victor Baldridge, Frank R. Kemerer, and Associates

9. Strategic Planning, Management, and Decision Making
   Robert G. Cope
10. Organizational Communication in Higher Education
    Robert D. Gratz and Philip J. Salem

1982 Higher Education Research Reports

1. Rating College Teaching: Criterion Studies of Student
   Evaluation-of-Instruction Instruments
   Sidney E. Benton
2. Faculty Evaluation: The Use of Explicit Criteria for
   Promotion, Retention, and Tenure
   Neal Whitman and Elaine Weiss
3. The Enrollment Crisis: Factors, Actors, and Impacts
   *J. Victor Baldridge, Frank R. Kemerer, and Kenneth C.
   Green*
4. Improving Instruction: Issues and Alternatives for Higher
   Education
   Charles C. Cole, Jr.
5. Planning for Program Discontinuance: From Default to
   Design
   Gerlinda S. Melchiori
6. State Planning, Budgeting, and Accountability: Approaches
   for Higher Education
   Carol E. Floyd
7. The Process of Change in Higher Education Institutions
   Robert C. Nordvall
8. Information Systems and Technological Decisions: A Guide
   for Non-Technical Administrators
   Robert L. Bailey
9. Government Support for Minority Participation in Higher
   Education
   Kenneth C. Green
10. The Department Chair: Professional Development and Role
    Conflict
    David B. Booth

1983 Higher Education Research Reports

1. The Path to Excellence: Quality Assurance in Higher
   Education
   *Laurence R. Marcus, Anita O. Leone, and Edward D.
   Goldberg*
2. Faculty Recruitment, Retention, and Fair Employment:
   Obligations and Opportunities
   John S. Waggaman

3. Meeting the Challenges: Developing Faculty Careers
   Michael C. T. Brookes and Katherine L. German
4. Raising Academic Standards: A Guide to Learning Improvement
   Ruth Talbott Keimig
5. Serving Learners at a Distance: A Guide to Program Practices
   Charles E. Feasley
6. Competence, Admissions, and Articulation: Returning to the Basics in Higher Education
   Jean L. Preer
7. Public Service in Higher Education: Practices and Priorities
   Patricia H. Crosson
8. Academic Employment and Retrenchment: Judicial Review and Administrative Action
   Robert M. Hendrickson and Barbara A. Lee
9. Burnout: The New Academic Disease
   Winifred Albizu Meléndez and Rafael M. de Guzmán
10. Academic Workplace: New Demands, Heightened Tensions
    Ann E. Austin and Zelda F. Gamson

1984 Higher Education Research Reports

1. Adult Learning: State Policies and Institutional Practices
   K. Patricia Cross and Anne-Marie McCarten